Other Titles in the Smart Pop Series

Taking the Red Pill
Science, Philosophy and Religion in The Matrix

Seven Seasons of Buffy
Science Fiction and Fantasy Writers Discuss Their Favorit~ T~

Five Season~
Science Fiction and Fantasy Writers

What Would Si~
Race, Rights and Redem~

Stepping through t~ ~~gate
Science, Archaeology and the Military in Stargate SG-1

The Anthology at the End of the Universe
Leading Science Fiction Authors on Douglas Adams'
Hitchhiker's Guide to the Galaxy

Finding Serenity
Anti-heroes, Lost Shepherds and Space Hookers in Joss Whedon's Firefly

The War of the Worlds
Fresh Perspectives on the H. G. Wells Classic

Alias Assumed
Sex, Lies and SD-6

Navigating the Golden Compass
Religion, Science and Dæmonology in Philip Pullman's His Dark Materials

Farscape Forever!
Sex, Drugs and Killer Muppets

Flirting with Pride and Prejudice
Fresh Perspectives on the Original Chick-Lit Masterpiece

Revisiting Narnia
Fantasy, Myth and Religion in C. S. Lewis' Chronicles

Totally Charmed
Demons, Whitelighters and the Power of Three

King Kong Is Back!
An Unauthorized Look at One Humongous Ape

Mapping the World of Harry Potter
Science Fiction and Fantasy Authors
Explore the Bestselling Fantasy Series of All Time

The Psychology of The Simpsons
D'oh!

The Unauthorized X-Men
SF and Comic Writers on Mutants, Prejudice and Adamantium

WELCOME TO
Wisteria Lane

On America's Favorite
DESPERATE HOUSEWIVES

EDITED BY
Leah Wilson

BENBELLA BOOKS, INC
Dallas, Texas

BenBella Books, Inc.
6440 N. Central Expressway, Suite 617
Dallas, TX 75206
www.benbellabooks.com
Send feedback to feedback@benbellabooks.com

Printed in the United States of America
10 9 8 7 6 5 4 3 2 1

Library of Congress Cataloging-in-Publication Data

Welcome to Wisteria Lane : on America's favorite desperate housewives / edited by Leah Wilson.
   p. cm.
   ISBN 1-932100-79-2
   1. Desperate housewives. I. Wilson, Leah.

PN1992.77.D49W45 2006
791.45'72—dc22

2006003171

Proofreading by Jessica Keet and Stacia Seaman
Cover design by Melody Cadungog
Text design and composition by John Reinhardt Book Design
Printed by Victor Graphics, Inc.

Distributed by Independent Publishers Group
To order call (800) 888-4741
www.ipgbook.com

For media inquiries and special sales contact Yara Abuata at yara@benbellabooks.com

Contents

Leah Wilson

Why America Is Desperate
for *Desperate Housewives*

INTRODUCTION

P ART OF WHAT I DO for BenBella every fall is size up the new television season and figure out which shows we need to pay attention to: which are likely to become hits, which are likely to have enough to them to sustain a whole volume of essays. Basically, which shows have the right combination of appeal and substance to make a good Smart Pop book.

Desperate Housewives was one of those shows that had "potential hit" written all over it, just by virtue of the marketing dollars ABC was putting behind it. But what surprised me, as I watched, was how much there was to say about it—how smartly done it was, for all its allegedly soapy allure, and how faithfully, if satirically, it reflected the (admittedly narrow) swatch of the modern female experience it had chosen to tackle.

When we were first discussing the idea of doing a book on *Desperate Housewives* in our office, our production manager, and the project's most vocal proponent, was Meghan Kuckelman, now a grad student in nineteenth-century literature. On Mondays, before the rest of the staff arrived for our weekly production meeting, Meghan and I would get together and "ohmigod!" about the night before's new episode.

"I can't believe it was Andrew in the pool," Meghan would enthuse.

"I still can't believe Susan bought what Mike said about shooting himself in the stomach," I would confess, nearly giddy, back.

While I'm a sucker for a good genre novel—sf, fantasy, mystery, romance, whatever—Meghan's reading tastes tend more toward Jane Austen and Emily Dickinson. I had designed my entire college curriculum

1

to avoid literature written before the mid-1900s, and Meghan was applying to go back to school and study it. In an office where the closest thing we have to a dress code is "make sure you're wearing clothing," I came in wearing heels as often as flip-flops, where Meghan preferred twice-repaired Birkenstocks.

But we both loved *Desperate Housewives*. And we were—obviously— hardly the only ones. The show is a runaway hit, lauded by critics and viewers alike. Particularly in the first few months the show was on the air, talk of the series was as pervasive as the latest reports on the Iraq war; *Desperate Housewives* was, in a sense, the ultimate domestic issue. And like the war in Iraq, the show united us in interest if not in opinion on the issues the series raised: infidelity, parenting, suicide, ADD... the list goes on.

Something about the show has succeeded in appealing to viewers across every demographic—despite featuring a handful of largely white, upper-class housewives in the suburbs who look really, really good for their respective ages. The essayists in this volume take on the task of puzzling out why.

Some of them attribute it to the strength of the characters, and their relationships with one another. Alesia Holliday couldn't help relating to Lynette Scavo's experience of motherhood. Michelle Cunnah fell in love with Susan, naïve optimism, dubious relationship schemes and all. Evany Thomas was struck by the appeal of the show's tried-and-true group structure—how often women's real-life friendships develop along similar lines, and how much we enjoying seeing friendships like our own on the television screen.

Others point to the show's technical proficiency. Lani Diane Rich thinks it's the show's stellar writing: the clever quips, the way the writers have made us love characters we started out hating. Jill Winters agrees, and presents as evidence the progressive emasculation of the show's male characters, cleverly set up in the pilot episode and played out masterfully during the whole first season. Nancy Herkness looks to the production design, and finds the details of each Housewife's home to be as revealing as any of her actions.

But the show also taps into deeper themes. Cara Lockwood notes the appropriateness of the show's suburban setting, long the backdrop of choice for all sorts of dangers both physical and psychological. Sarah Zettel, in exploring *Desperate Housewives*' appeal to men, reveals the American cultural myths that the series first draws on, and then explodes.

And that's just the tip of the ice sculpture.

So welcome to our trip down Wisteria Lane. You'll never look at *Desperate Housewives* the same way again.

The Good of the Group

Desperate Housewives was billed as Sex and the City's older married cousin: a girlfriend show, but with husbands, kids and a soapy suburban setting. Critics knew Sex and the City's end had left a hole in the viewing lives of women across the country; what they missed, and what Television Without Pity's Desperate Housewives recapper Evany Thomas gets, is that Sex and the City itself was only the most recent in a long line of shows that capitalized on viewers' delight in seeing themselves, and their friends, reflected on their television screens.

THIS MORNING I woke up late. After the world's fastest shower, I threw on some clothes, smeared lipstick in the direction of my face, reached to flush the toilet, and...WHOOSH! My face, hair, clothes and entire bathroom were instantaneously drenched. Apparently the water had been turned off in my building during the night, thereby booby-trapping an explosive air bubble in my pipes. As I stood there, dripping in the wake of a toilet geyser that had doused my hair, face and clothes, I heard the distinct sound of my cat vomiting in the hall behind me.

It was not my best moment. Unfortunately, it wasn't my worst moment, either. My life has been a series of spectacularly klutzy episodes. I have accidentally set fire to a rug, a car and a coffeemaker—all on separate occasions. I've coated an entire kitchen with a fine layer of refried beans and covered a first date head-to-toe with ketchup. I was there for both the San Francisco earthquake of 1989 and the Los Angeles earthquake of 1994. Wherever I go, birds tear hair from my head to use as fodder for their nests and strange men with misplaced pants try to hug me. Also? I was born with a pair of "ironic ankles": thick and sturdy in appearance, they topple without the slightest provocation, priming the pump for a lifetime of pratfalls, spilled drinks and sudden disappearances.

And why? Why am I the subject of so many unpleasant accidents, mishaps and disasters? Because I, I am a Susan. I may not have a charming teenaged daughter, or illustrate children's books, or live in Suburbia, but at our core bubbles the same fundamentally spastic quality. And we both have an amazing, tight-knit group of beautiful, brainy and funny female friends.

My friends even have their own Desperate Housewife twins. My friend Liz loves champagne, Prada mules and sparkly jewelry, just like Gabrielle. And every once in a while, a little Edie peeks through: at dinner the other night, we all got to talking about how many people we'd each slept with, and Liz said, drolly, "There isn't enough ink in the world for my list." Meanwhile, my friend Jill has a touch of Bree in her: she bakes perfect cakes which she presents on perfect cake pedestals, she washes all her T-shirts by hand so as not to fade the color and she always, always, always sends a thank-you note.

And just like the Desperate Housewives, my friends are always there for each other. They're ready with high heels and champagne whenever one of us has something to celebrate. They're available day and night, via phone, e-mail or instant messenger, to help analyze every last detail and puzzling nuance of each friend's fluctuating love life. And they're front and center with ears open, shoulders free and frosted foods in hand whenever bad news arrives, just as Susan, Gabby and Lynette were there for Bree when Rex went into the hospital with his second heart attack:

MARY ALICE (in voice-over): It was five o'clock in the morning on Wisteria Lane when the phone calls started.

(One by one LYNETTE, SUSAN and GABBY wake up and answer their phones.)

MARY ALICE (in voice-over): Of course each of them knew something was wrong from that first ring. After all, it's one of the unwritten rules of Suburbia: don't call the neighbors in the middle of the night unless the news is bad. And so they came, with their un-combed hair and their unmade faces—they came because, after all these years, they were no longer just neighbors. ("Goodbye for Now," 1–22)

This amazing availability, this willingness to rush to the scene of hurt like white blood cells to a wound, is just one of the many things that makes watching groups of female friends such compelling entertainment.

Certainly comedians have made much ha over the fact that women can never go to the bathroom alone. This female "clumping instinct" also leads us to travel in packs to bars, outlet malls and amusement parks. And we share everything: clothes, perfume, the most intimate details of our life…everything. So for pure voyeuristic fun, groups of women make for lively viewing. But the appeal of a close-knit group of female friends goes deeper than the surface entertainment provided by the basic instinct to clump. A true group friendship between women is a rare and complicated thing. There's a synergy there, with the whole of the group somehow adding up to more than the sum of what each individual player has to offer. And it's pure Hollywood gold.

Groups of women have been the framework for all kinds of successful movies and television shows. Sometimes the women are related by something as unshakeable as blood (as seen on *Sisters* or the new 2005 WB show *Related*) or as tenuous as happening to have been born from women who took the same birthing class (*The Sisterhood of the Traveling Pants*). Or they attend the same school (*Divine Secrets of the Ya-Ya Sisterhood*, *The Facts of Life*), or work at the same job (*Designing Women*, *It's a Living*, the new 2005 show *Hot Properties* on ABC), or join the same band (*Josie and the Pussycats*, *Spice World*), or share the same occultish talents (*The Craft*, *Hocus Pocus*, *The Witches of Eastwick*), or date all the same people (*The L Word*). Or maybe their common ground is just that: ground, groups of women thrown together because they live in the same house, neighborhood or city (*Desperate Housewives*, *Sex and the City*, *Living Single*, *The Golden Girls*). The things that bring women together on the screen may seem artificial, but really the causes that unite us in real life are often just as random: My friends and I all met because one of them posted an ad for a roommate, and I happened to answer it.

The randomness of these connections guarantees that the feature players come to the friendship manned with vastly different backgrounds and experiences. Combining women who have very different ideas about clothing, decorating, dating, marriage and parenting not only makes for lively stories, but also guarantees dramatic clashes between characters. Also, the intermingling of characters, each with her own arsenal of strengths and weaknesses, allows the characters to help each other, and evolve and grow together as a group. All of which makes for some rich and varied television. But "different women united by slim circumstance" is only half of the formula. The shows and movies also have to feature the right combination of characters.

The secret to the success of *Desperate Housewives* is that it features characters that viewers relate to, and relate to passionately. My friends and I aren't the only ones who've found versions of ourselves mirrored in the show's stereotypes. Declaring an affinity for one of the Housewives has actually become something of a national pastime. On a local level, people are getting together at *Desperate Housewives* theme parties and declaring their affinities: Vermonter Kim Jennings, who creates maps of the supermarket aisles to make shopping trips easier, declared at a local Housewives culinary-sale party that she is very much a Bree.[1] And a reporter in Corvallis, Oregon, who recently wrote a "why we watch"-style Housewives story for her local paper, signed off as "Mary Ann 'I'm a Lynette' Albright."[2]

And people are letting their Bree (and Lynette, and Edie, and Susan, and Gabby) flag fly all over the Internet. The *Television Without Pity* "Like OMG We're Twins! Which DH are you?" discussion board[3] is full of posters telling the world "I'm a Bree" or "I'm an Edie." And that board is just one of many, many online forums providing a platform for similarly *Desperate* announcements: Fans are also sharing their not-so-secret identities on the official ABC boards, Atkins Diet support message boards, the Knitters Review boards, the Reality TV World boards, Soap Opera Central boards and the BabyCenter boards, just to name a few.

Even the actresses who play the Housewives themselves have their own affinities and opinions about how they stack up against the characters they play. Felicity Huffman says she very much relates to her Housewife, Lynette, but Marcia Cross claims to be nothing like Bree. Meanwhile Nicollette Sheridan, who plays Edie, says that she herself

[1] Pollack, Sally. "Kitchenware Party Would Make Bree Blush." *Burlington Free Press*, 17 May 2005 <http://www.burlingtonfreepress.com/specialnews/afterdark/>.

[2] Albright, Mary Ann. "Desperate Housewives Mid-valley Fans Speak Out." *Corvallis Gazette-Times*, 24 September 2005 <http://www.gazettetimes.com/articles/2005/10/01/lifestyles/family/fam01.txt>.

[3] "Like OMG We're Twins: Which DH Are You?" Discussion Forum. *Television Without Pity* <http://forums.televisionwithoutpity.com/index.php?showtopic=3119568&pid=2890851&st=75&#entry 2890851>.

identifies with a completely different Housewife: "I love home. I cook. I have the house very clean. I'm actually much more like Bree."[4]

People are even letting their chests advertise their Desperate Housewife affiliations: As a self-professed Susan, I can buy myself an "I'm a Susan" T-shirt for $24.95 off of ABC's official *Desperate Housewives* Web site. Or, thanks to an enterprising entrepreneur at Cafe Press,[5] all you Brees out there can purchase your own apron that advertises your Housewife double. Or, for more private declarations, interested parties can invest in "I'm a Gabrielle" thong underwear.

For those of you still unclear as to which Housewife you are, don't worry: the Internet is chock full of "Which Housewife Are You?" tests and quizzes to help you get in touch with your inner Housewife. All you have to do is answer some multiple-choice questions (for example: "In high school I hung out with…," "For breakfast I usually have…," and "I feel most desperate when…"), and soon enough you'll know the identity of your Housewife match. Or perhaps you already know which Housewife you are…you just know yourself under a different name.

Desperate Housewives isn't the first show to feature a group of women comprised of exactly these Types: "The Spaz" (Susan), "The Traditional Perfectionist" (Bree), "The Sarcastic Pragmatist" (Lynette) and "The Loose One" (Edie/Gabby). If the ladies of Wisteria Lane were to, for example, take one of the "Which *Sex and the City* Girl Are You?" quizzes (and there are many still available online, even though the show is no longer in production), Edie would discover that she is a Samantha, Susan would learn that she's a Carrie, Bree would be a Charlotte, and Lynette a Miranda. Similarly, a "Which Golden Girl Are You?" test (and again, there are many) would reveal Edie to be a Blanche, Susan a Dorothy, Lynette a Sophia and Bree a Rose (these last two characters being united more by their shared essence of traditional innocence rather than Bree's perfectionist bent). And of course all the ladies could buy themselves corresponding declarative clothing: "I'm a…" tees are available for the four characters of both the *Golden* and *Sex* shows.

The fact that we find such a similar grouping of these types of female characters reincarnated and re-reincarnated is no coincidence. Marc Cherry, the creator of *Desperate Housewives*, first worked on *Designing Women* (as personal assistant to actress Dixie Carter), before spending two seasons as a writer and producer for *The Golden Girls*, the grandmother of all the female-foursome shows. His next project,

---

[4] *People Magazine Extra, Desperate Housewives Edition*, October 2005: 58–61.

[5] Canadian Socialite *Desperate Housewives* Merchandise. October 2005 <http://www.cafepress.com/cdnsocialite/458018>.

the critically acclaimed (but almost immediately canceled) show *The Five Mrs. Buchanans*, featured four married women all struggling under the thumb of one nasty matriarch. (*Housewives* fans will recognize some of the names and faces from the show: One of the Mrs. Buchanans is named "Bree," and the character Vivian Buchanan was played by Harriet Sansom Harris, the actress who now plays Felicia on *Desperate Housewives*.) And then Cherry hit the big time with *Desperate Housewives*, which he has acknowledged was inspired in part by *Sex and the City*. Clearly Cherry was working from experience when he created the *Desperate Housewives* characters; his background with shows based around groups of the same kinds of female characters provided a blueprint for exactly the combination of characters that the public warms up to most.

This lineup—The Spaz, The Traditional Perfectionist, The Sarcastic Pragmatist and The Loose One—resonates with viewers in part because it's comprised of women we recognize both in ourselves and in the women who surround us. Yes, the Housewives are cookie-cutter cutouts of real women, but just as this Susan and her circle of Bree and Edie-like friends go to show, these sorts of women do exist in the real world, and they do indeed become friends. Stereotypes become stereotypes for a reason. That said, accessible stereotypes only go so far.

My friends and I are real, live people, which of course means we're far too messy and complicated to fit neatly into our corresponding Housewife boxes. We Susans have our Edie moments, Brees experience their share of Gabrielle cravings and Edies go through their Lynette phases. Our lives are unscripted, which means our personalities evolve, revert and adapt depending on the changes that befall us. We even have our own highly individual types and traits, the likes of which have never been seen on Wisteria Lane. *Desperate Housewives* may capture our attention initially by holding up a mirror and showing us characters we relate to, but ultimately that first blush of recognition breaks down. After that, it's the way these women interact with each other that keeps us tuning in week after week.

The true beauty of the Desperate Housewives (and the Golden Girls, and the *Sex and the City* women) is the way these characters fit together. Bree is the moral compass of the group, but she's also a demonstration of what it costs to get too sidetracked by appearances; Edie and Gabby remind the group to have fun but not to let things get too carried away; Lynette voices what everyone is afraid to say out loud; and Susan is the bumbler with a battered heart who reminds her long-married friends how rough the search for love can be. Like the wedge and the Pacmanish circle in one of my favorite childhood books, *The Missing Piece*,[6] each Housewife's unique characteristics, skills and experiences fill in the holes created by the other characters' weaknesses and lapses. Each woman is an expert in her own "field," and as such, she is available as a specific resource to each of her friends. Take this scene from "Fear No More" (1–20) where Lynette, whose husband had been hiding the reappearance of an ex-girlfriend, sought advice from Edie:

LYNETTE: Look, you're basically a predator and I need your advice.

(EDIE looks intrigued. Cut to LYNETTE and EDIE, who are mid heart-to-heart.)

LYNETTE: And I know Tom loves me, but I don't trust this woman. I think there's an agenda there. I don't know, maybe I'm being paranoid.
EDIE: No, no. You did the right thing by coming to me. There are two ways to approach this. Well first I have to ask, what kind of shape is this woman in?
LYNETTE: Fantastic shape. She's gorgeous.
EDIE: Okay, now there's really only one way to approach this. You're going to have to act fast.
LYNETTE: I'm listening.
EDIE: Well, it's really pretty simple. When I feel threatened by a woman, I pull her in. I make her my best friend.
LYNETTE: I thought you said you didn't have any female friends?
EDIE: I don't. And I've never felt threatened by another woman either. But the point is, keep your friends close...
LYNETTE: ...keep your enemies closer.

The Housewives help and complement each other, but their friendships can also be complicated and hard, full of conflict, growing pains and plenty of drama. Susan and Edie clash jealously over men, Susan disapproves of Gabrielle's relationship with the oh-so-young-and-tender Gardener John, Bree disapproves of Lynette's lax parenting and Lynette isn't the biggest fan of Bree spanking Lynette's kids. Yet still the friends remain friends, demonstrating how conflict can be a way for each character to expand her horizons or, at the very least, discover the new empathy that comes from seeing an unquestioned

---

[6] Silverstein, Shel. *The Missing Piece*. HarperCollins, 1976.

assumption from a different point of view. Plus all the snarking and car-versus-roller skates battles are a whole lot of fun to watch.

But whether they're fighting or helping each other out, these characters are always a pleasure to watch interact. The times that *Desperate Housewives* most falters as a show are when it neglects to bring its characters together in any meaningful way. During the episodes where the characters keep to their separate orbits, with no interaction with the other Housewives, the characters seem two-dimensional, and the flaws and limitations of each woman's stereotype start to glare. But when the characters meet up to exchange some hot gossip or to stage an intervention, they come alive and the show truly soars.

Unfortunately, the Housewives' only regular, reliable connection is their poker game, which from what little we've seen appears to be operating on a schedule that's entirely too sporadic. Perhaps the ladies should follow the lead of my group of friends: for the past ten years we've been getting together once a week for "TV Night." Every Sunday we share an evening of good food, fine company, comfortable clothing and horribly glorious television. For years we watched *Sex and the City*, and then, when that show retired, we switched to *Desperate Housewives*, alternately yay-ing when the characters kiss or achieve one of their small successes and groaning sympathetically whenever the ladies indulge in some foible we recognize all too well.

Wouldn't it be perfectly awesome if the Wisteria ladies had a TV Night of their very own? Every Sunday night they would come together to eat pizza, catch up on each other's lives and yell at the television as it played some gloriously titillating show about a group of gorgeous, brainy and hilarious female friends: one Spaz, one Sarcastic Pragmatist, one Traditional Perfectionist and a Loose One.

Evany "I'm a Susan" Thomas writes the *Desperate Housewives* recaps for *Television Without Pity*. She's also the author of *The Secret Language of Sleep: A Couple's Guide to the Thirty-Nine Positions*, the "Tyrolian Harvest" sausage basket catalog in *McSweeney's* Issue 17, plus a variety of articles (covering everything from rare cars to soothsayers) for a variety of Web sites (including *MSN*, *Webmonkey*, *Breakup Girl* and *The N*). More about her writing, history and day-to-day activities can be found at Evany.com.

Evelyn Vaughn

Why I Hate Lynette, and How That Could Be a Compliment
Maybe. Kind Of.

The best television shows are the ones in which we recognize something of ourselves in the characters. But that doesn't mean we have to like what we see. Forget imitation; for Evelyn Vaughn, the highest form of flattery may actually be hate.

'VE WATCHED *Desperate Housewives* now, faithfully, through the first season and into the current second. Clearly, I enjoy it. And yet, one thing constantly surprises me.

Wow, I sure do hate Lynette.

Mind you, I like the actress, Felicity Huffman. I've said it before and will say it again—the actor is not the character, although the two can be intricately linked. I can't imagine another actress doing any better with Lynette than Huffman does, so I'm not blaming her. Way to go with that Emmy award, Felicity!

But Lynette? The woman drives me crazy, and not in a good way. Susan may be an absolute klutz. Bree may be a control freak. Gabrielle cheats on her husband with a teenager, for heaven's sake! But it's Lynette Scavo who makes my teeth ache, week in and week out. And, to judge by people on some of the TV discussion sites, I am not alone.

And what's really weird? Our hatred may be the biggest compliment we could pay her.

Maybe.

Kind of.

Let me explain....

The Fine Line Between Love and Hate...

If you've spent much time on television forums, like *Television Without Pity*, where viewers post opinions about the latest episodes of favorite shows, you may have noticed an interesting phenomenon.

Some people seem to take real pleasure in hating particular characters, or even entire shows—and then talking about it at length.

A large number of *The O.C.* viewers seem to hate Marissa lately. Plenty of *Gilmore Girls* viewers dislike Rory and despise Logan. Me, I very much like Mischa Barton's Marissa Cooper, Alexis Bledel's Rory Gilmore and Matt Czuchry's Logan Huntzberger (actually, I adore him). So I've gone from bewilderment to condescending excuses for the people who continually complain about them. In some cases, the viewers may be jealous by proxy, wishing the romantic pairings had gone to other characters...or, in fan fiction worlds, to *them* (come on, don't deny it, it's true for at least a few of you). Sometimes these characters, for whatever reason, seem to cast a pall over a show the dissidents otherwise honestly love. Hey, I get TV love. I can understand the frustration. There's a reason an official method of "jumping the shark" is the introduction of a "New Kid in Town." Scrappy-Doo, anybody?

Then there are the viewers who take glee in posting, about everything from *7th Heaven* to *Charmed*: "I hate this show," or "When will they cancel this piece of junk and put us out of our misery?" or "Kill me, kill me now." This, I do not get. It's as if the posters are looking for a fight, the way people who call into shock-jock radio shows to make noise and stir up trouble might, rather than wanting to voice honest concerns. Me, I wouldn't wish a show cancellation on any fan, since I can always put myself out of my own misery by *changing the channel*.

And yet, I haven't changed the channel on *Desperate Housewives*, despite my violent reaction to one-fourth of the main cast members. I don't fast-forward through the Lynette scenes. I'm not sure I even see her presence as casting a pall over an otherwise great show, because Lynette really is an integral part of the *Desperate Housewives* dynamic.

So what's up? The only way to get past my Lynette hatred and see the perhaps-surprising explanation on the other side, I'm afraid, is to go through it.

Lynette Creates Her Own Problems

Here's the first thing I truly dislike about Lynette: Almost everything that goes wrong in her life is something she helped engineer. Don't believe me?

She didn't have to have four children—one (or, in the case of the twins, two) could be an accident, but in this day and age of birth control (and her uppercut when her husband suggests they "risk it" without birth control, in the pilot), surely she could have avoided four. She didn't have to agree to quit the corporate world and become a stay-at-home mom. Whatever the pressure that was once on her, *she* chose these things.

Her biggest problem—that her boys are hellions—is at least partly the result of her lax discipline. True, there's scant room for comparison with two of her fellow housewives, here. Gabby doesn't yet have children (and deliberately so, might I add). And while Susan may not be much better as a disciplinarian, she was blessed with Julie, the perfect daughter, so we can't tell. But then there's Bree. Bree's hit-and-run, old-lady-killing sociopath of a son, Andrew, is no poster boy for good behavior. But at least Bree makes an active effort to curb his bad behavior. In "Who's that Woman?" (1–4), Bree realized Andrew had snuck out to a strip club—and went right after him. After frightening away his friends, she sat with her son to comment on the show.

> BREE: I'm curious, Andrew. As you fantasize about this woman, do you ever stop and think how she came to be on this runway? That's someone's little girl. And that someone probably had a lot of dreams for her. Dreams that did not include a thong and a pole.

When that beautifully delivered guilt trip didn't work, Bree took a page from Dr. Laura Schlessinger herself and removed the door from Andrew's room. She's making the effort.

Lynette, on the other hand, has little follow-through when it comes to her boys' discipline. In "Children Will Listen" (1–18), Lynette threatened her children with a spanking, only to then throw a fit when Bree—whom she dumped them on at the last minute—did in fact spank one of them. Her argument *started* with: "Tom and I don't believe in hitting our kids. I thought you knew that." So . . . why did Lynette threaten a spanking in the first place?

Heck, consider the pilot episode. In one of Lynette's very first scenes, we were meant to see her cunning mind when she told the boys to behave or else—and showed them what she claimed was Santa's phone number. "I know someone who knows someone who knows an elf. And if any of you acts up, so help me, I will call Santa and tell him you want socks for Christmas. Are you willing to risk that?"

Hee. Clever. And yet what happened? The boys did misbehave (this was at Mary Alice's wake, mind you), and Lynette made the disruption even bigger by wading into the pool to drag them out, and *did we see her making the threatened call to Santa?* No, we did not.

In "Who's that Woman?" (1–4), Lynette was called to school because the twins had painted Tiffany Axelrod blue. She told their teacher, "Well, obviously they will be punished for this. Severely." But did we see her punishing them, severely or otherwise? No, we did not.

And in "Love Is in the Air" (1–14), Mrs. McClusky accused Lynette's boys of stealing a clock her now-dead son had made for her, and how did Lynette respond? "Are you sure you didn't misplace it? You're getting up there in years. No offense, but you probably forget where you put things." Despite fairly obvious evidence, she had to be brought face-to-face with her sons' ill-gotten gains before she admitted that, surprise, they really were thieves! So come on. Do we really believe that she had no hand in how these boys turned out, even if her sin was mainly that of omission?

No, we do not. Or at least, I don't.

That was only the start of Lynette's self-made problems. Nobody forced those first few Ritalin pills down her throat—she got herself addicted. She managed to hire a great nanny, but because of her own insecurities—and her unwillingness to enforce a few extra rules—fired her and went back to complaining about how she was always stuck at home with the children. Which leads me to the second reason I dislike Lynette....

Lynette Complains. A Lot.

Oh good heavens, does Lynette complain. It was there from the start, in the pilot.

Lynette, nursing her infant: "Ow! Ease up, little vampire."

Lynette, leaving a message for her husband: "Tom, this is my fifth message and you still haven't called me back. Well, you must be having a lot of fun on your business trip. I can only imagine. Well, guess what, the kids and I wanna have some fun too, so unless you call me back by noon, we are getting on a plane and joining you." (Note: This is yet another empty threat.)

In contrast, Susan complains a little—usually about her ex-husband. Gabrielle rarely complains, except to her husband, and when that doesn't work, she takes a lover instead. Bree hardly ever complains, even when she's got cause to, even when she probably should (poor, repressed Bree). But Lynette? In episode 14, we were treated to a series of cuts in which she was complaining about suffering through the ugly handmade gifts her children give her, wishing she could get one she wasn't embarrassed to display! Poor, poor Lynette, suffering through the amateur art of *her children*!

When a policeman pulled her over for allowing her children to jump around the car, rather than making them wear their seatbelts, her response was: "I have no help, my husband is always away on business.... My babysitter joined the witness relocation program. I haven't slept through the night in six years.... And for you to stand there and judge me!"

Isn't that kind of a policeman's job, when he sees a dangerous situation?

True, to people Lynette wants to impress, she'll say of being a mother, "It's the best job I ever had." According to the Mary Alice voice-over, that's a lie. To anybody whose opinion doesn't matter, it's another story. In "Every Day a Little Death" (1–12), Lynette showed up late for a yoga class and therefore couldn't get childcare. Her response to the clerk's refusal was as follows:

> LYNETTE: Uh, Lauren? I'm a mother of four. Today I had to get up at five, make lunches, make breakfast, drop the twins off at school and get across town lugging a baby and a sick child. Telling me to plan ahead is like telling me to sprout wings.

Which brings me to. . . .

Lynette Is Selfish

Did you catch the most telling little detail in Lynette's last rant, the kind of detail most mothers catch immediately? She came to the yoga class "lugging a baby *and a sick child*." Yep, Lynette was not only angry because she couldn't leave her children in childcare, since it was full up, but because she couldn't leave her *sick* child there, where he could get the other children sick.

Nice one, Lynette. Especially considering that you then let the same clerk believe your son was dying of cancer, in order to take advantage of said childcare.

Now, Lynette's by no means at Andrew Van De Kamp level, pure sociopath selfish. She brought fried chicken to Mary Alice's wake. She clearly cares about her friends. But neither is Lynette particularly skilled at considering others before herself—perhaps we're supposed to see this as the mark of a good businesswoman?

In the pilot episode, in the supermarket, her boys rammed a shopping cart into a little old lady. Lynette's reaction? She was *embarrassed*. No matter that a broken hip can be something akin to a death sentence to a senior citizen. *People were staring at her*.

When she left her husband to care for the boys while she attended the Van De Kamps' dinner party, she gave the oldest a box of cookies. "Tonight, anything goes. Make sure you share with your brothers" ("Pretty Little Picture," 1–3). Passive-aggressive much?

When lecturing her sons about having stolen from their old next-door neighbor, she said, "You stole and then you lied. Even worse? You made me look bad in front of Mrs. McClusky, who you know is Mommy's sworn enemy."

Nice way to prioritize there, Lynette.

In "Come in, Stranger" (1–5), Lynette begged Bree to recommend her twins for the prestigious Barcliff Academy. "Tell them how beautifully behaved the boys are." Bree protested that she didn't want to lie: "It's just that I'm very well respected at Barcliff, and my word won't be good there anymore."

LYNETTE: Yes, but by the time they realize their mistake we'll be in.
BREE: Well, I had hoped someday to get my grandchildren into Barcliff. But I suppose that doesn't matter to you, does it?
LYNETTE: It really doesn't.

And do I even have to point out that Lynette poached a desperately needed nanny, Claire, from her secure job by making extreme offers, only to then fire her? Claire was an excellent nanny. That was the cause of Lynette's initial dislike for her—she was *too* good, better with the boys, in fact, than Lynette. But Claire was caught running naked through the house in the middle of the night to throw her robe into the dryer, and Lynette's husband was turned on by that, so she was gone. I'm not saying Claire made a good choice, there. But because of Lynette, she lost not only her job at the Scavos' but the excellent job she originally had, from which Lynette lured her. As long as Lynette need not worry that her husband finds other women attractive, it's a small price to pay, right?

And on the bright side, at least Lynette was able to then complain about not having a nanny for the rest of season one.

Certainly Lynette is not the only selfish housewife of the quartet—a certain Gabrielle Solis comes to mind. But Gabby is blatant about her selfishness. Proud of it, even. As with Edie Britt, there's something strangely honest about Gabrielle's deceptions. Compared to Gabby and Edie, Lynette seems merely petty. And compared to the far more selfless Bree and Susan, Lynette looks even worse.

And finally (really, the gripes are almost over):

Lynette Is Not as Advertised

We're told by Mary Alice and other, more alive, characters that Susan's something of a sweet-natured goofball, and sure enough, that's Susan. Gabrielle is apparently a sexy woman who likes to spend money—other than the fact that she must have been the shortest runway model in all of fashion history, that works too. Bree is one of the "perfect housewife" types who bakes muffins and polishes silver, right? And while she takes it to extremes...check.

So how often are we told that Lynette was a corporate wizard? The old colleague she met in the supermarket, in the pilot, told her flat out, "We all say, if you hadn't quit, you'd be running the place by now."

Lynette stated at one point that she ran a company of eighty-five people, and at another point that she made more money before she quit than her husband, Tom, did even then, many years later. When she poached Nanny Claire from an already great job, Lynette supposedly managed it because of her excellent business skills. And toward the end of season one, lunching with an old colleague, Lynette tried to feel her out about a job for Tom (to get him away from his ex-girlfriend/current co-worker). At first the colleague thought Lynette was in the market for a job, and begged her to come back to work. When Lynette tried to sell Tom instead, her disappointed colleague asked, "Is he as good as you?"

Of course, he is not. So Lynette convinced her old colleague to hire Tom's more ruthless ex-girlfriend instead. When Tom lost a promotion because of Lynette's scheming, and quit in protest, he agreed to an earlier proposal Lynette made: *He* would be the stay-at-home parent, and *she* could go back to work.

I don't know about other viewers, but I celebrated. "About time!" I shouted at the television, scaring my dog. Man, I hated Lynette, with her overall incompetence at mothering and her continued disappointment with said incompetence. I was ready to see corporate mastermind Lynette!

But what happened at the start of season two?

Lynette was reduced to working for a boss who refused to accommodate her children, her hours or her home life. Lynette had to miss her child's first morning of school—for a morning staff meeting, mind you, not an emergency trip to New York or something. She had to stay out every night for a week helping her boss hook up with one-night-stands, all apparently for...fear of losing her job? She has been as put upon as ever, just in a different environment!

That doesn't sound like a corporate wizard to me. That does not make me think "shark." Instead, it sounds like the same kind of wimpy woman who rarely says no to her husband and can't control her own children, and I've been no more impressed with her second season than I was with the first.

So...How Can Any of This Be a Compliment?

But here's the weird part of my whole diatribe against Lynette. Remember what I said at the start?

I enjoy the show. I don't even fast-forward through the Lynette scenes. So what *really* bugs me so much about this woman, even more so than Susan's continued incompetence or Gabrielle's statutory rape of her underage gardener, John?

I've realized that what really bugs me is—Lynette is the most original, most realistic of any of the housewives. She's almost *too* real. And that makes her threatening to the average, escape-seeking viewer.

Think about it. The sweet but goofy Susan Mayer is a familiar TV character. She's like Lucy Ricardo meets Mary Richards. Can't you just imagine her intoning, "Oh, Mr. Grant!"

Bree, of course, is transplanted directly out of the age of *The Adventures of Ozzie and Harriet*, *Father Knows Best*, *Leave it to Beaver* and *The Donna Reed Show*, complete with sweater sets and pearls. Especially *The Donna Reed Show*, now that I think of it, what with the doctor husband, one daughter and one son. Mrs. Donna Stone made cookies from scratch too, you know. (No wonder Bree has trouble with issues like her husband's sexual fantasies or her son's possible homosexuality. These things simply did not exist in the TV world of Donna Reed).

Gabrielle is familiar from a more recent period of television, what Tim Brooks and Earle F. Marsh, in *The Complete Directory to Prime Time Network and Cable TV Shows*, would label the ABC Fantasy Era of the early '80s. You know the kind of show I mean, don't you? *The Love Boat. Fantasy Island. Dallas. Dynasty. Falcon Crest.* That and, of course, soap operas.

But Lynette...?

I don't know about you, but I'm drawing something of a blank. Stay-at-home mothers we can still spot on TV now and then, but many of those are still surprisingly like Bree in surface behavior and appearance. (Marion Cunningham, of those old *Happy Days*, even had the sweater sets—and Marge Simpson, on *The Simpsons*, wears pearls). Corporate women we see plenty of nowadays, but few of them either can afford to leave their jobs (Roseanne Conner) or are willing to leave their jobs (Murphy Brown) to raise their children. Some, like Ellenor Frutt in *The Practice*, not only insist on their ability to have a child while working full time, but then bury themselves so heavily in their job that the character of their baby sort of slides away into the mists of lost TV characters, simply... forgotten. In movies, I suppose we've got the example of Diane Keaton's character in *Baby Boom* (followed by a failed sitcom of the same name, starring Kate Jackson). At least that gives us the corporate-woman-turned-mother. But there are as many differences as similarities. In *Baby Boom*, the heroine has a child dumped on her—she doesn't give birth herself—and she uses her corporate skills to flourish, after only a little comedic floundering, in her new role. Or, to bring it back to more recent TV, there's always Debra Barone from the award-winning *Everybody Loves Raymond*. But unlike Lynette, Debra is a competent mother, far more frustrated by her in-laws than her children.

A woman who gives up her corporate position for full-time motherhood, only to decide that she was better in the corporate world? Only to learn upon getting a second chance that no, she's kind of floundering there, too? Who feels ambiguous about her love for her children, torn as she is by an equal resentment of what they've done to her life?

Really, I can't think of one. For all my hatred, Lynette really is an original. She's more *real*...which, considering rumors that she (like Bree) was loosely based on creator Marc Cherry's own mother, would certainly make sense. (My apologies, by the way, to Marc Cherry's mother—this is about Lynette, not you!)

And that, my friends, might neatly explain just how badly she bugs.

At the risk of pure psychobabble, isn't there a theory that we are most annoyed by those qualities which we see and dislike in ourselves? By being real, Lynette holds a mirror up to the average viewer's average flaws. Hopefully, few of us can claim to be as consistent a klutz as Susan, or as strict a control-Nazi as Bree Van De Kamp. And I seriously hope few of us cheat on our spouse with the underage help, like Gabrielle. Those three housewives simply don't threaten us...well, don't threaten me, anyway.

But Lynette?

Surely I'm not the only person who has ever feared she created her own problems, and then disliked herself for it. I hope I'm not the only one who feels sorry for myself, or is sometimes selfish. And surely I'm not alone in that niggling fear that I'm not as good as advertised! Am I?

If I am alone in all this, then that at least explains why I dislike Lynette.

But if—as I suspect—I am not, then it may explain a lot of the other griping going on across online forums every Sunday night. Lynette is frustrating because *humanity* can be frustrating. Her flaws are human flaws and, might I add, not typically female or male. In some ways, Lynette is the person many of us fear becoming. For that reason, we hate her. Or do we?

Because we certainly keep coming back for more!

The author of over a dozen romance/adventure novels, Evelyn Vaughn is not a wife, nor is she particularly desperate—but she does own a house. Happily single, she divides her time between writing and teaching English at Tarrant County College SE in Arlington, Texas. She is unlike all four of the main characters in *Desperate Housewives*... but will admit a loose resemblance to Mrs. Frome. You know. The one with the cat. And she hopes to grow up to be more like Mrs. McClusky.

In the meantime, Evelyn is an unapologetic TV addict. She's still trying to figure out how to time travel or meet up with some of her favorite characters. Check out her Web site at www.evelynvaughn.com.

Ritalin, Rivalry and the Rat
Lynette and Desperate Motherhood

Unlike Evelyn Vaughn, Alesia Holliday found in Lynette a welcome reflection of her own life, and her own personal struggles. More than a desperate housewife, Lynette was a desperate *mom.*

T HE IDEA of a new TV comedy-drama-soap about desperate housewives didn't do much for me, since I've never once in my life been a housewife. From the days when I ran a business during the day and went to law school at night, to the time when I was a practicing trial lawyer with two children under five and a husband gone to war after September 11, there was never any "housewife" in my job description. I wasn't interested in watching a TV show about women with whom I had nothing in common.

The buzz got to me, though, as buzz so often does. I took a quick peek at the show's first episode, met Lynette Scavo, and I was hooked. I could ignore the "housewife" part. Lynette was a desperate *mother*, and oh, wow, pass the diaper and hold the existential angst, could I empathize with that. I wanted to watch the show almost in spite of the other characters. (Well, except for that hot plumber. Let's not forget him....)

Gabrielle? Nope. No kids, no job, nothing in her life but shopping. Not my cup of tea.

Susan? Her teenaged daughter was a more active parent than Susan was. Nothing to catch my interest there.

Bree? Martha Stewart meets B-movie psychotic. The woman probably irons her *sheets*. Cringeworthy, sure, but not enough to keep me watching for an hour.

But then there was Lynette, in all of her frazzled glory. The sole character who'd sacrificed her career to motherhood and demonstrated on a daily basis just what a painful sacrifice it had been. The sole character whose very existence was representative of the dual fronts of the most brutal Mommy Wars, and she was scarred but not defeated, battle-weary but not ready to surrender.

The truth is, she had me from day one of season one, when the beaten expression of abject despair on her face told us that she knew she'd lost her identity.

She'd lost her purpose.

She was close to losing her mind.

Been there, done that, have the breast-milk-spit-up-stained T-shirt to prove it.

Lynette's struggles exemplified the unglamorous reality of motherhood in all its desperate glory: the sacrifice—of self, sanity and, yes, let's admit it, sex life; the thoroughly modern conundrum of how exactly we're supposed to "have it all, be it all, do it all" and somehow make it to Mommy and Me class with hair and makeup intact. I couldn't look away.

Supermom Gone Wild

Lynette's background as a talented and ambitious advertising executive did absolutely nothing to prepare her for life as a stay-at-home mother. Most aspects of her old life had no place in her new one.

The personal digital organizer didn't have quite the same functionality for scheduling breast feedings and play dates as it did for slotting in client presentations and business lunches. Not to mention that, without a secretary to remember to provide fresh batteries on a regular basis, that expensive PDA becomes a dust-covered paperweight lost somewhere in a basket piled high with six-month-old issues of the *Wall Street Journal*. The thousand-dollar suits weren't really the thing to wear to the grocery store or preschool. And the superwoman, Type A, hard-charging attitude that made her the best of the best?

Finally. Here's the part of the package unaffected by Lynette's new reality, in her mind. She could simply transfer her ambitious nature to her parenting role.

Unfortunately, this is never a good idea.

One character trait ubiquitous among female executives is the need to excel in all areas. Never let 'em see you fail. The idea of coming in second-best is as horrific to a supermom as it is to a super career woman (SCW). Lynette's very identity was wrapped up in her career, and in order to establish her new identity, she had to prove that she was, yet again, Queen of the Hill: she needed to have the best damn costumes in the preschool.

The problem with transferring exalted expectations of success from the business to the parenting world is that the support system does not transfer with the goals. A woman who is accustomed to twenty-four-hour word-processing services, a team of support personnel and—most unrealistic of all—people who listen to her and do what she asks will be blindsided by the realities of stay-at-home motherhood.

The days where it's suddenly five o'clock in the afternoon, and she hasn't even had time for a shower.

Babies with colic who cry unreasonably loudly for unreasonable amounts of time and unreasonably refuse to sleep.

The total brain-frying exhaustion that only utter sleep deprivation can cause. (Note to Lynette: Some less-enlightened regimes actually torture prisoners with sleep deprivation. That nap you need so desperately? It's no luxury to take it. More like a necessary element of survival.)

But when an unstoppable SCW meets the immovable reality of motherhood, does she scale down her unrealistic expectations accordingly?

Of course not! That's what Ritalin is for!

When Lynette's friend turned her on to the joys of recreational Ritalin use, she believed she'd found a miracle in a bottle. Those pesky costumes? No problem! She stayed up all night to finish them, and they turned out *great*. The disaster of a house? No problem! An entire cleaning team couldn't match Lynette on an artificial high.

But when she hit bottom, walking away from her children and falling down in the middle of a grassy field, the only thing that helped was the truth about supermoms: that nobody really is one. Bree and Susan shared their stories of how difficult parenting young children was for them, and Lynette turned to them in tears and asked: "Why didn't you tell me this before?"

The truth is, nobody talks about how hard it is. The truth is, too many women are caught up in the SCW trap, or captured in the never-ending cycle of depression, hopelessness and hostility sometimes called Mommy Guilt.

Mommy Guilt

Intrinsic to the inherently impossible "I'm the mother, so I must always be right" expectation comes the reverse side of the coin: "When I'm not right, I need to feel guilty about it."

And mothers certainly do. It's the all-guilt, all-the-time channel. 24/7 of we're not doing enough, doing it right, doing it best. If a husband dares to suggest a different or, God forbid, possibly *better* way of doing something, he needs to be slapped down.

Hard.

Case in point: When poor Lynette was desperate to attend Bree's dinner party for a break from her chaotic week with the kids, Tom refused to go with her. He'd been out of town "working hard" (as evidenced by the sombrero and margarita pictures; amazingly she saw them but still let him live). When she decided to go to the party without him, she tried to give him childcare instructions. Tom responded flippantly, with "they're just kids; it's not rocket science."

To Lynette, this was an unforgivable mistake: He belittled her very existence with a single sentence. His dismissive tone and words told Lynette that what she worked daily to accomplish wasn't valued by her husband: that the role of parenting, the one she struggled to excel at, was a job that was worth *less* to Tom than his own corporate job.

Since Lynette is more of an action gal than a pop-psychology adherent, she didn't sit Tom down and explain that his words caused her to believe that her self-worth was on the line. She didn't tell him that by diminishing her role as a parent, he undercut the basis of the new identity she'd tried so hard to create.

Nope. Not Lynette. She told the kids to eat all the cookies they wanted. We call it "sugaring up" the children. Lynette calls it justice.

The Mommy Wars

In the very first episode of *Desperate Housewives*, I empathized so much with Lynette that I put the show on my "must watch" list. When she rounded that corner at the grocery store, disheveled and exhausted, with her boys acting like monsters, and ran into a former colleague, I nearly cried for her.

Because I've been there. I've been the one with breast-milk leakage issues, still carrying an extra twenty pounds from pregnancy, wearing ugly gray sweatpants and an old flannel shirt, carrying a screaming, colicky baby, when I ran into a former colleague.

It's never somebody you *like* when that happens.

"How are you enjoying motherhood?" they ask, with a sickeningly sweet "oh, how she has fallen" smile.

When Lynette's face froze, and she gritted out, "It's the best job I've ever had," I knew exactly what she was feeling inside.

(Sadly, homicide-by-canned-goods is illegal in most places.)

When an SCW turns to full-time motherhood, the ugly specter of cognitive dissonance enters the picture. She begins to wonder what's wrong with her. But she tells herself, "It's my choice, damnit. I *must* be happy, I chose this."

She doesn't allow herself the "frivolous self-indulgence" of needing time to adjust to the transition. The SCW expects to launch into super-momhood as she did everything else in life: going full-speed ahead.

Instead, she often finds herself, by default, on what she used to consider the "wrong" side of the Mommy Wars. The former SCW has both poles of the stay-at-home mom versus working mom debate all wrapped up in one fresh, lemon-scented person.

Her new acquaintances, women she meets at baby play groups and the park, loudly opine on the doom awaiting the children of working women. Terrible parenting, you know. Quantity versus quality is a bad joke. Everyone knows that a child needs her mother.

Right?

On the other side of the tug-of-war are her former colleagues. They call and e-mail to keep in touch at first, but with less and less frequency as time goes by because they don't quite understand why all she can talk about is how often the baby pooped. She's not as interested in office gossip. She usually has to hang up to deal with a screaming baby. And everyone knows that the brain of a career woman who stays home with a baby turns to mush.

Right?[1]

Unfortunately, the mother trapped in the middle of two completely different value systems is also trapped by her own unrealistic expectations. She wonders why she is not happy at all times and completely fulfilled by her children. Felicity Huffman, the actress who plays Lynette (and has two children of her own), is quoted in the *Washington Post* as saying: "There's one way to be a mother, and that's basically to go, 'I find

---

[1] This would be the place, if this were a different essay, where the author would question the convention wherein class differences come into play. In other words, why is the middle-class mom applauded for staying home and vilified for going to work, and yet the poverty-level mom is a hero for getting a job, and a leech upon the system if she stays home with her children? Standards for good mothering as defined by your tax return?

it so fulfilling, and I've never wanted anything else, and I love it.' And if you do anything that diverges from that, you're considered a bad mother. I didn't know this existed until I became a mother, and the pressure is phenomenal."[2]

As if *any* mother, whether stay-at-home or career woman, needs more pressure.

Right?

Supermom Goes Back to Work

Sometimes, the parameters change. Supermom goes back to work. Financial necessity or personal choice dictates a return to the corporate world. In Lynette's case, her constant scheming and manipulation wound up getting her husband fired. Some men would have divorced her over it. Tom decided the best revenge was to send her back to work. He'd be the stay-at-home parent.

How hard could it be?

Supermoms who return to the workforce face a terrible dilemma: How can they still be the "best" parent when they're only parenting part time? Even when—maybe *especially* when—Tom suddenly had the most one-on-one time with their children, Lynette was driven to prove her superiority. Because, after all, she is the *mother*.

In Lynette's mind, Tom doesn't:

- keep the house clean enough
- watch the children carefully enough
- do anything well enough

And she doesn't hesitate to let him know she thinks so. When he disagrees, she must prove him wrong. By any means, fair or foul.

Even if she has to sacrifice a pet-shop rat to do it.

When Tom's lax housekeeping left the house looking like vagrants had swarmed though it, he refused to bow to Lynette's requests that he clean it. He had different standards. He had a "schedule." She needed to "relax."

So she bought a rat and let it loose in the house. When she returned from work that day, the house was spotless. The boys reported that they'd found a rat. Tom admitted defeat. She was right; he was wrong.

---

[2] *WashingtonPost.com.* "The Truths of 'Desperate Housewives," Ellen Goodman, Nov. 20, 2004, p. A19.

It was the sweetest praise Tom could have given her.

The perhaps unintentional symbolism of Lynette's trash can came into play here. During her conversation with the rat, as it lay dead inside the trash can, she lauded the sacrifice it had made for her happy home. The act of throwing the rat in the trash can itself might reflect the sacrifice Lynette made of her scruples in order to achieve the greater good.

If Lynette would go to that kind of length to prove she was a better parent than Tom, there was no way an *umbrella* was going to get in the way. Her son's imaginary friend, as represented by the umbrella, didn't last long. Lynette went back to the trash can, this time with the umbrella; her status as uber-parent remained undefeated.

Finally, if a clean house was worth the rat subterfuge, what price was Lynette willing to pay to ensure her children's safety? When Lynette came home from work after dark and found her boys playing in the street, with no parental oversight by Tom, she was furious. But Tom failed to appreciate the enormity of his transgression. He told her he was doing fine.

Lynette wasn't going to let that go unchallenged: In her mind, *she* is the parent who defines "fine" for the Scavos. She asked the receptionist from work to try to entice the children into his car, simply to prove to Tom that she was right, and he was wrong. (There was the fact that the children were not safe enough, as well, but the issue of her status as "best parent" is never far from Lynette's mind.)

Manipulation is simply another tool in the parenting tool belt for Lynette. She'll manipulate Tom without a qualm. And the boys? Well, let's just remember that she has Santa's e-mail address.

When Lynette came up against a foe she couldn't easily manipulate, her self-proclaimed "childless by choice" boss, the sparks flew and the viewers watched in breathless anticipation. Lynette will always prevail because she's a fighter. We know this about her, and we were itching for the showdown (or the bar dance, as it turned out). Lynette's methods may be messy or underhanded, but in her view the simplistic norms of traditional thinking don't apply to the working woman with children.

On the other hand, her boss had a valid point. Why should childless colleagues have to pick up the slack for the parents who need time off for child-related activities? Since nuances of social issues are generally beyond the scope of an hour-long television show, *Desperate Housewives* went the easy route and demonized the boss. She was a bitch on wheels. She didn't understand or care about Lynette's desire to attend her son's first day of school. She was a slutty tyrant, and she got what she deserved when Lynette got her fired.

Except... *except*. Except maybe the boss devolved into who she was because of the demands of the job. Except maybe Lynette was in for trouble with her new relationship with the ultimate boss, who seemed to be a demanding child himself.

But that didn't faze Lynette when she took the offensive in the Great Day Care Skirmish. When a desperate mom returns to the workforce, the ends don't just justify the means, but become Holy Grail–like in their perceived urgency. Lynette *would* gain more time with her children. The firm *would* have a day care.

And so she did. And it did. And we watched and cheered, in spite of any doubts we may have harbored about her methods. After all, she is us. We have to be on her side.

Desperate moms on both sides of the stay-at-home versus work-outside-the-home divide have found a champion in Lynette. She'll continue to dance on the sharp edge of the Diaper Genie, sometimes coming out smelling like a freshly powdered baby and sometimes falling into the muck, and we'll watch, empathize and love her for it.

But we won't *sympathize*. Lynette wouldn't want our sympathy.

Super Mommy—like me, like so many of us—is one tough broad.

Alesia Holliday's first book was all about being a desperate housewife. The autobiographical *E-mail to the Front* was the first book to tell the real truth about military families when one spouse is at war. After several years as a trial lawyer, Alesia is a "recovering" attorney turned award-winning author. For news of her novels—romantic comedies, chick-lit and mysteries—please visit her online at www.alesiaholliday.com. For news of her latest Desperate Mom moment, you can visit her blog and laugh at her. (Everybody else does.)

Alesia, who in her college days was a lot like Gabrielle, is now firmly in Lynette's camp. Except Alesia's kids are way, *way* better behaved. And there are no rats.

Growing Up Wisteria

If we've learned anything from the women on Wisteria Lane, it's that mothering is a tricky business, liable to drive you to anything from abandoning your kids on the side of the road (if only temporarily) to treachery, deceit and, in Mary Alice Young's case, out-and-out murder. Beth Kendrick surveys Desperate Housewives' most high-profile mothers, and asks the question every parent fears: What are these people doing to their kids?

THE MOTHERS OF WISTERIA LANE have one thing in common—they all love their kids more than anything. And they all believe that if they just tried a little harder, they could be the mothers their children deserve. But Bree, Susan and Lynette have widely disparate family dynamics and child-rearing philosophies, and the more they strive for parental perfection, the more desperate they become.

I have a theory about this, actually: as the outfit goes, so goes the mothering. Although I have no idea whether the *Desperate Housewives* wardrobe department collaborates with the writers, the show excels at telling us everything we need to know about each character with a well-placed accessory, a loose button, a stain from baby vomit. We have Susan, who wears tie-dye tank tops and crotch-length lamé cocktail dresses like a trendy teenager; Bree, who dresses like her own grandmother in twin sets and pearls; and Lynette, who opts for the no-nonsense masculinity of khakis and baggy Oxford shirts. All three are happy to make sacrifices—hell, Mary Alice was willing to *kill*—for their children, but the moral of this show is there's no such thing as the perfect parent. With motherhood goes great responsibility...plus rage, despair and danger.

Let's take a closer look at the mothering styles on Wisteria Lane. How do the three main characters handle the pressures of rearing children in an idyllic suburban neighborhood roiling with secrets and betrayal?

Character: Susan Mayer
Parenting Style: Parenting? What parenting? We're BFF—more like sisters!
Outlook: Raising Bree Van De Kamp, the next generation

Susan, honey, we need to talk.

I know the last few years have been tough sledding, what with the breakup of your marriage, your smarmy ex-husband moving in with your nemesis and your attempts to find true love with the hunky, heat-packing plumber across the street thwarted time after time.

But take a look around. Doesn't someone else live in this house with you and all your neuroses?

That's right: Julie. YOUR DAUGHTER.

From the moment we first saw her in the pilot episode, Julie was the de facto adult of the Mayer household. Julie made sure the bills were paid while Susan fell apart after the divorce. Julie arbitrated the custody conflicts between her mom and dad. Julie consoled Susan after the breakup with Mike and helped orchestrate their reconciliation.

Julie is a freshman in high school.

While Susan acts like she's forty going on fourteen, Julie actually is fourteen. She needs to feel secure enough to make mistakes and start establishing independence.

In the pilot episode, Susan refused to discuss her sex life with Julie (good call), claiming that it "weirds me out." But by the end of the season, she broke down and agonized with Julie about how to seduce Mike and whether she should agree to have his children, then invited him—an admitted felon—to move into her house without even running it by her daughter. Susan also enlisted Julie's help in: infiltrating a mental institution, reading a criminal file detailing Mike's history of drug dealing and manslaughter, breaking into Mrs. Huber's house to steal back the charred measuring cup and arranging a ride home after a date went sour.

In the second season, she became so crazed with jealousy when Julie planned to perform at a church concert with Edie that she stormed into Edie's house, announced that she played a mean piano and demanded that Julie choose between her and Edie. After Julie succumbed to the guilt and chose Mom, Mom interrupted the recital—leaving Julie alone onstage, staring back at a whispering audience—to hash out her differences with Edie right then and there.

And then she wonders why Julie has such bad taste in men.

Susan's sole solid parenting decision was to keep Julie away from the tightly wound ambassador of angst also known as the boy next door. But here's the thing: Julie was probably drawn to Zach because he reminded her of her mother—needy, damaged, desperate to be rescued. After fourteen years with Susan, Julie is accustomed to the role of perpetual caretaker and emotional anchor. She's more than attached; she's enmeshed. It's only natural she should transfer this behavior from the familial arena to the romantic.

Yes, Susan is an artist and is very expressive, imaginative and emotionally open. These are all good qualities, in moderation. But involving your child in your every romantic whim and paranoid urge to snoop? It's called impulse control, babe. Seriously. There's a time and a place. Time and a place.

So how might Julie turn out as an adult? Well, I'm voting for Bree Van De Kamp version 2.0. Julie's temperament is inherently different from her mother's—whereas Susan craves drama and excitement, Julie prefers stability. She was probably one of those infants who slept through the night at eight weeks and never refused to eat her carrots. But, as Bree demonstrates, too much self-control can be a bad thing. Bree confided to Zach during their impromptu holiday dinner that her mother died when she was "very young." So, essentially, she grew up motherless, with little parental guidance and an increasing need to impose order on a chaotic world. Bree's obsession with appearances stems from the fact that she has no idea what's really driving her psychologically. She creates the "ideal" family as an adult because her childhood was so unpredictable. Sound like anyone else we know?

What's really interesting about Susan's BFF approach to parenting is that she should know better. Susan had it even worse than Julie did—her mother Sophie is a ditzy, serial-marrying party girl. Given that Susan and Sophie would have ended up living in a cardboard box if they had *both* been as flighty as Sophie, we have to assume that Susan was on bill-pay duty, etc., as a child. So why has she grown up to be an even more accident-prone (and we all know what Freud said about accidents!) version of Sophie? Maybe she's now living out the adolescence she never had. Maybe the burden of responsibility traumatized her. Maybe she's doing it unconsciously to exact payback from Mom. Whatever—it's a vicious cycle, and can't she please snap out of it before Julie matures into the next candidate for "mayor of Stepford"?

Character: Bree Van De Kamp
Parenting Style: Iron fist in a velvet glove
Outlook: Don't make any sudden moves

Say what you will about Bree—you have to admit she's consistent. She's raised her two children with well-defined boundaries and punishes them for their infractions. She has a very strong sense of right and wrong, which she's tried to instill in her son and daughter (with mixed results). There is no confusion in the Van De Kamp household as to who is the parent and who is the child—Bree was willing to kick down her son's bedroom door, track him across town to a strip club and initiate a heart-to-heart about family values while strippers gyrated in the background. And she's not afraid to hug her children, say "I love you" or talk frankly about sex, drugs and what Jesus would do.

So why did Andrew end up in a far-flung boot camp for juvenile delinquents, only to return with a burning vendetta to "destroy" his mother?

Bree faces two major obstacles to raising well-adjusted children: her husband and her lack of self-knowledge. You can make a pretty convincing argument that the reason Bree's teenagers are so rebellious, resentful and, in Andrew's case, downright scary is that her co-parent never backed her up. Adolescents are surly by nature, but Rex exacerbated the problem. He was erratic, to put it mildly, first ignoring his children's outward displays of disrespect toward Bree, then encouraging them (by buying them a car and enrollment in a modeling academy when he left their mother), then losing his temper and threatening to "put [Andrew] through a wall." The kids had no idea what to expect from their father on any given day. Though Bree specifically referred to Rex as "the head of this household," she was always more competent, more level-headed and more ballsy than he.

In a way, Rex was Bree's third child. He couldn't make up his mind about anything: he loved her, he hated her, she was a great mother to his children, she was a horrible mother to his children, he wanted a divorce, he wanted to give the marriage another shot, and on and on and on. After the unfortunate salad bar incident, Rex accused Bree of being cold and unfeeling—"perfect" in the worst sense of the word—but he himself was so capricious and sulky that he didn't leave his partner a lot of room to be spontaneous. Someone had to step up and hold the family together, and Bree was the only one willing to do the job.

When Rex moved out of the house to have an affair, the children blamed Bree for "driving my father away." This illuminated two key family issues. One, the children saw Bree as Rex had cast her—prim, proper, and relentless in her quest to keep up appearances at the expense of emotional honesty. Two, the children felt safer blaming Bree. Mom was the secure parent—Andrew and Danielle could express hostility to her and feel confident that she would still love them. Rex was dicier. His affections ran hot and cold, and he wasn't one to get worked up about his children doing...well, anything, really, which telegraphed the message that he wasn't all that invested as a father.

Bree lives for her family, but she's also very into surfaces. Her hair and clothing. How clean her kitchen floor is. What the neighbors will think. She couldn't leave the house until her bed was made, even though her husband was doubled over from a heart attack. Yet she's not superficial—she cares deeply about her children and her principles. She's adamant that Andrew and Danielle adhere to the same strict moral code and punishes them when they don't (e.g., when Andrew smoked marijuana, she alerted school authorities and got him kicked off the swim team.) So why, when her son drank, drove and ran over Juanita Solis, did Bree go to such lengths to cover for him? Screw the lofty morals; suddenly, she was a criminal mastermind. Given the fact that her own mother was killed by a careless driver, you'd expect her to have a zero-tolerance policy for that sort of thing.

I see two possibilities as to why she decided to cover up for Andrew's hit-and-run. One, she was overcome with resurfacing grief over the loss of her mother and refused to let a car accident rob her of yet another family member. Two, she never really dealt with the loss of her mother and could not bear to face the emotions that threatened to engulf her when Carlos' mother was taken from him, just as her mother was taken from her. When Bree recounted her mother's death to Zach, she said that she was too young to accompany her father to the hospital and was left at home. The sight of her mother's blood on the asphalt so disturbed her that she dragged out the hose and washed the street, which relieved her panic and despair. And *voila*, a world-class housekeeper was born!

Ever since her mother died, Bree's been polishing and scrubbing and pruning instead of wrestling with life's sordid realities. So by covering for Andrew, she was continuing to sublimate the grief she'd never been able to face. She headed right over to the Solis house to scrub the asphalt again, this time with a can of industrial-grade solvent. And then, when Andrew showed no remorse for running down "an old lady" who had "already lived her life," Bree got upset that he excelled at maintaining a façade, even though that's what she'd modeled for the children her whole life. Mama's boy or soulless sociopath? Only time will tell!

Character: Lynette Scavo
Parenting Style: Utter freaking chaos
Outlook: Not bad, actually

Poor Lynette. She tries so hard. And as an advertising exec, she's used to reaping lucrative results from her efforts. But while logic, threats and steely-eyed stare-downs get you what you want with white collar employees, they have little to no effect on six-year-old boys. In a way, Lynette is the most rebellious of the Wisteria Lane moms: She doesn't do Pottery Barn parenting. No trendy child-rearing books in her house. The woman doesn't have time to obsess about co-sleeping or organic baby food or psychologist-approved high-contrast mobiles. She's too busy trying to hold her ground in her daily battle of wits with three sons so wily that they will probably grow up to start their own special ops military division.

The character of Lynette lets us glimpse the seedy underbelly of parenting: the highs, the lows, the unrelenting mess that comes with cultivating new life. Her sons lie, steal, bite, bully other children…and yet, even as they push her to the edge, they fill her with delight: "You're the best mommy in the whole world." They are her curse and they are her salvation.

Lynette has the most masculine energy of the Wisteria Lane moms. She's not one to back down from a challenge and would rather roll up her sleeves and duke it out with a rival PTA mom than waste her energy on petty, passive-aggressive power struggles. She can go head-to-head with any man and come out on top, and is justifiably cocky about her abilities. But her sons are her Achilles heel—they expose her to criticism and the naked terror of failure. "Why can't you control your kids?" was a constant refrain throughout the first season, and part of Lynette's emotional journey is accepting the fact that she *cannot* control them. They are exotic, willful strangers who gang up on her to achieve their own goals. As Tom points out, once the children outnumber the parents, it's all over.

The attributes that make Lynette such a fabulous businesswoman are the same attributes that sandbag her as a mother: her drive for excellence and her keen sense of rivalry. She knows that the neighborhood perceives her as substandard at her "job" and sees herself as falling helplessly behind her competition: Bree and Susan. After the combination of stress, insomnia and recreational use of ADHD medication left her fantasizing about suicide, Lynette confided that she felt sorry for her children because they got stuck with her for a mother: "I used to run a company with eighty-five people and now I can't wrangle three young boys without doping them" ("Who's That Woman?" 1–4).

Lynette told her husband that "my mom used to beat the hell out of my sisters and me" and she vowed she wouldn't do the same to her children ("Children Will Listen," 1–18). However, her mother's abuse seems to have scared Lynette out of any consistent approach to discipline; we never see her employ a time-out, but apparently threatening to beat her kids with a belt is a-okay as long as she doesn't actually follow through. The only tactic left to Lynette is psychological warfare, and she's practically Sun Tzu of the Baby Einstein set. After Bree spanked one of the Scavo boys, Lynette used the threat of Mrs. Van De Kamp as her muscle. She let a sympathetic gym employee assume her son had cancer to secure him a place in the facility's childcare center. When Tom was fired but refused to keep the house clean, she planted a rat in the living room to spur him to action. An innocent rodent had to die, but hey, there are always a few civilian casualties. Overextended and underappreciated, she finds ways to get what she needs. Work smarter, not harder!

In the midst of all the subterfuge and one-up-manship, though, is a cohesive family. Lynette and Tom relate to each other as friends and their boys, for all the mischief, are basically loving, confident kids. Lynette has a sense of humor and playfulness that Bree lacks, which keeps her sane (barely) even as her world disintegrates before her eyes.

So what's a mom to do? We have three devoted mothers, all determined to provide their children with the very best, and all convinced that they've failed their families on the most fundamental levels. If only Lynette could pass on some of her confidence to Susan, if Susan could imbue Bree with some of her expressiveness, if Bree could instill her flair for organization in Lynette. Parenting looks so easy from the outside (Mary Alice was positive that she could be a better mother than the drug-addled Deirdre, and look how Zach turned out), but as the residents of Wisteria Lane's immaculate homes have discovered, there's no such thing as a perfect mother. Everyone knows that but no one accepts it, driven wild by their desperation to achieve that particular (sub)urban legend.

> Beth Kendrick has a Ph.D. in psychology and three poorly parented dogs. She covets Gabrielle's wardrobe and Edie's personal trainer. Beth's novels include *Fashionably Late, Exes and Ohs* and *My Favorite Mistake*. You can visit her Web site at www.bethkendrick.com.

Is Suburban Living Hazardous to Your Health?

If there's anything in Suburbia that's going to kill you, it's likely to be the boredom. So why are fictional 'burbs such hotbeds of sex, murder and other middle class mayhem? Cara Lockwood has an explanation or two.

WHEN I TOLD some of my single friends that my husband and I were planning to buy a home in a suburb of Chicago, many of them shook their heads sadly and said, "Your life is over."

To them, leaving the city was a self-induced exile, away from all things that matter. Moving out to the suburbs meant exchanging the excitement of city living for weekends of mowing lawns and shopping for SUVs. It meant ample parking, but no theater, indie movies or food more exotic than pizza.

But on television, suburbs are *it* in terms of excitement. Wisteria Lane on *Desperate Housewives* is one neighborhood in a long line of tales from television Suburbia, where sex, murder and intrigue rule. There's Seaview Circle (*Knots Landing*) and Pine Valley (*All My Children*), and even on the show named for a city (*Dallas*), the principal action happened away from the city limits on Southfork Ranch, located in the real suburb of Plano, Texas.

TV's latest suburban neighborhood, Wisteria Lane, has seen its share of excitement. In just two seasons, we've witnessed a suicide, a murder, an elaborate cover-up, a prostitute arrest, a torrid affair, white-collar crime, blackmail, a kidnapping and, oh yes, a mysterious man held captive in the basement of a new neighbor's house. By all accounts, there's nothing as exciting happening in the big city as in this one-block stretch of street.

So it makes sense that I approached my move to the suburbs with some trepidation. Would I find myself living next door to a couple who had killed the birth mother of their child? Or would my neighbor be secretly having an affair with a teenage gardener? It turns out that, as far as I know, my neighbors don't have any of these secrets. In fact, if attending the Neighborhood Association meetings are any indication, they are, actually, the most boring people on earth. The biggest drama to hit my block in the last month was a very heatedly debated sewer renovation project which redirected traffic from our street for two weeks. Second to that is an ongoing feud between my two neighbors involving the use of a shared patio.

Don't get me wrong. An affair with the gardener might be a good idea, except that none of them in my neighborhood look like Jesse Metcalfe. And believe me, I have certainly contemplated murder, especially when a contractor came to my house to renovate my kitchen, and went six weeks longer and $5,000 over budget. But as far as I know, the only serious crime in my block involved a guy getting a ticket for doing a rolling stop at the corner stop sign, and he didn't even live around here.

I don't think there are any torrid affairs going on at all, but I could be wrong. At any rate, I do know that "last call" at our neighborhood restaurant is at 10 P.M., so there would definitely be no place for Edie Britt to pick up men.

But despite the severe lack of action in my little corner of Suburbia, my neighbors do seem to be constantly on the lookout for it.

What I have found about suburban living is that people seem a lot more interested in your business here than in the city. City neighbors rarely exchange more than two words at a time. Casual hellos, but little else, for fear that if you get to know someone well and find out you don't like them, there's only about two feet of space between your condo and theirs. It seems like there's almost a mutual understanding: You leave me alone, and I'll leave you alone, and we'll live in this building together in peace.

But the suburbs are different. One of my friends, who recently moved west of Chicago, found herself and her husband invited to a number of neighborhood barbeques this past summer. And at every one, people she'd barely met started asking her and her husband, who have no children, "So, when are you guys having kids?" She got so tired of the personal nature of the question, that she started asking back, "When was the last time you had sex?"

This, naturally, mortified her husband, but she would just shrug and say, "What! If they can ask such a personal question, I can ask one, too."

Needless to say, I don't think either of them has been invited to head up the Neighborhood Watch.

So why is it that television always makes the 'burbs a more exciting place to be than they really are?

One theory is that it's just a bunch of TV executives hoping to placate the millions of us that have traded exciting city life for big supermarket parking lots and Blockbuster rentals.

"We don't want to believe we've lost anything by moving out to the suburbs," says one of my friends, who recently gave up city life for quick access to Wal-Mart and Target. "And you know TV. They glorify everything."

Case in point: On TV, people who live in New York have spacious, trendy apartments bigger than my house, when in reality only Donald Trump can afford something that roomy. Most normal New Yorkers live in efficiencies and pay $2,500 per month for the privilege. There's no possible way that the *Friends* folks could've afforded their apartments. Not unless one of them has access to a large trust fund.

And TV is notorious for making life seem more exciting in general. If you were an alien life form trying to figure out humanity by TV, then you'd certainly make the mistake of thinking that there's far more sex, murder and one-line quips than in real life. Oh, and most of us are size zeros, and have perfect makeup and hair at all times. My personal favorite are the shows where the wives (like *Everybody Loves Raymond* and *King of Queens*) are supposed to be unglamorous, but still manage to come off as trendy, sleek and stylish. It's got to be all those hair products.

So making suburbs more glamorous than they really are just fits in with how TV treats all subjects, from law firms to hospitals. But is there more at work here?

In *SuburbiaNation: Reading Suburban Landscape in Twentieth-Century American Fiction and Film*, Robert Bueka argues that in many works of fiction and film the suburbs are depicted as anything but utopian. The idea of danger and dysfunction lurking behind the pristine lawns of Suburbia are common to many images of the 'burbs in fiction and film.

In fact, we have long had an uneasy relationship with the suburbs, not quite sure whether we love them or hate them. One of the earliest references to this ambivalence in fiction, Bueka argues, is Sinclair Lewis' *Babbitt* published in 1922, a story set in the smallish city of Zenith and the equally unremarkable suburb of Floral Heights.

Bueka writes, "[T]he struggle of Lewis' protagonist, George F. Babbitt—between conformism and rebellion, domesticity and adventure, civic pride and a sense of entrapment—set the blueprint for subsequent representations of male suburbanites."

The suburbs, Bueka points out, have long represented a kind of nowhere land, stuck between rural and urban America, neither completely private nor completely a community.

So, it's clear we aren't quite sure what to make of the suburbs. In the 1950s, they promised a new utopia, offering cheap and bountiful housing to soldiers and their families after World War II. These returning soldiers sought stability, family and conformity, which suburbs provided in spades. We see this today in many of our suburban neighborhoods. Houses and lawns conform to a strict set of Neighborhood Association rules, and people who don't adhere to them are socially ostracized, or worse, taken to court. People living in the suburbs are typically thought to be more politically conservative, more likely to have children and more likely to commute to work by car.

But as much as the suburbs are about community, they are also about privacy. City living by and large has people living in very close quarters, in condos and apartments, sharing public spaces like hallways, foyers, sidewalks and yards. The suburbs gave people more privacy than they'd ever had—individual houses and yards, and the primary mode of transportation is private cars, rather than walking on sidewalks or sharing buses or trains.

Lynn Spigel, a Northwestern University Radio/Television/Film Professor who wrote *Welcome to the Dreamhouse: Popular Media and Postwar Suburbs*, is an expert in media studies and post-war television and film, and discusses the balance of private and public in suburban life. In the suburbs, Spigel writes, "[T]he family could mediate the contradictory impulses for a private haven on the one hand, and community participation on the other."

But we are a pretty nosy species as a whole. How did we adapt to this newfound privacy? Clearly, some of us, like the gossipy neighbors in every neighborhood (such as poor deceased busybody Martha Huber), didn't do so well. We didn't like the artificial barriers the suburbs placed between our lives and others. We wanted to know what was going on behind closed doors. Television provides a glimpse into other people's lives without us actually having to get into our neighbor's business. After all, be honest, would you really want to know if your neighbor had a body buried under his swimming pool?

Given the fate of Martha Huber, I'm guessing not.

So in one sense, TV gives us a way to peek behind the curtain, allowing us to be nosy without offending our own neighbors in our own communities.

So we want to live vicariously. That's fine. That explains the soap opera drama and torrid love affairs. But why, then, are suburbs on television so very dangerous?

On Wisteria Lane, at the end of season one, the body count already stood at five: Mary Alice (suicide), Martha Huber (bludgeoned with blender), Gabrielle's mother-in-law (hit by car, before slipping on the hospital stairs), Bree's husband (poisoned) and Zach's birth mother (stabbed). And that was only on one street. I wonder what's happened in the rest of the subdivision.

Could it be that secretly we *do* think suburbs are dangerous? That despite our attached garages, our playgrounds and our better schools, we honestly believe there's something sinister about living in a cul-de-sac?

Ironically, there are real dangers to suburban living. They just aren't the sexy kind. Obesity, car accidents and lawn chemicals are just some of the dangers lurking in Suburbia.

Take commuting, for example. Urban sprawl is the catch phrase of urban planners, who have spent years tracking the cost to us, both in time and money, of living in the suburbs. Since 1982, the time Americans spend in traffic has jumped 236 percent, according to *U.S. News and World Report*. In major American cities, the length of the combined morning and evening rush hours has doubled, from under three hours in 1982 to almost six hours today. The average driver now spends the equivalent of nearly a full workweek each year stuck in traffic. And sitting in traffic costs Americans more than $78 million a year in wasted fuel and lost time, thirty-nine percent more than in 1990.

Furthermore, commuting is exacting a toll not only on our bank balances, but on our bodies. Suburbanites tend to be more overweight than their urban counterparts, and more out of shape, according to the National Institute of Diabetes and Digestive and Kidney Diseases. This is due in large part to spending so much of our free time sitting in our cars. Obesity, of course, is projected to surpass smoking as the leading cause of preventable death in the United States as soon as this year.

And if getting fat doesn't kill you, just getting into your car could. Every year there are 43,000 fatal car crashes in the United States, and the more time you spend in the car, the greater your odds of finding yourself in one.

The Sierra Club's recently posted "10 Reasons Sprawl is Hazardous to Your Health" includes the above reasons and a few others, including pollution—both from our cars and from our houses—which are exacting a toll on our health. New houses going up every year means we're polluting our own water supply by building over 100,000 acres each year of pollution-absorbing wetlands. For proof of a more imminent danger of building on wetlands, look at New Orleans. The expansion of suburbs there over water-absorbing wetlands contributed to the massive flooding and death toll after Hurricane Katrina.

Suburbanites also might be at risk for more rare diseases than urban dwellers, thanks to the spread of neighborhoods into wooded areas. Lyme Disease has soared from 120 cases annually to almost 18,000 in the past twenty years, according to the Biodiversity Project and the Lyme Disease Foundation. And if that's not worrisome enough, the Sierra Club tells us, suburbs could be toxic, as our pristine green lawns are treated with more pesticides per acre than croplands, exposing us to toxins that could cause cancer and damage our neurological and reproductive systems.

And here's something else to think about—if you do get into an accident or collapse from exposure to toxic lawn chemicals, you might die because you live too far away from a hospital. Many suburban centers are awfully far from the trauma centers of big-city hospitals.

So we're not exactly likely to be bludgeoned to death by a blender, but we *are* likely to die of cardiovascular disease or a car accident simply by not being able to get treatment in time.

Then again, let's rethink death by blender.

Violent crime, the thing many of us flee when leaving urban centers, seems to be slightly on the rise in Suburbia, while it's in decline in the cities. A report from the Federal Bureau of Investigation in 2002 showed a 1 percent increase in violent crime in U.S. suburbs in 2002, compared with the previous year. The same report also found a 1.9 percent drop in violent crime in urban areas and a 1.2 percent decline in rural areas in 2002.

All in all, Wisteria Lane seems like a safer place by the minute, compared to the dangers in our own real-life suburbs.

But that isn't stopping us all from moving there in droves.

Cheaper housing, more room for raising our families (my friends with babies have said they moved to the 'burbs for the closet space alone) and the draw of better schools have thousands of us moving there every year.

For many of us, suburban living is a necessity, but one we're not sure we are quite ready to embrace. It's practical—ample parking, cheaper housing and more closet space—but what are we giving up in exchange for comfort and convention?

But maybe the real dangers lurking in the suburbs aren't the violent kind, but the slow and perhaps even more dangerous assaults on our psyches.

Women, especially, have long had mixed feelings about the 'burbs. In the 1950s, of course, women flocked to the new suburban utopia along with their husbands. But by the 1960s and 1970s, the suburbs had become less of a utopia for women and more of a prison.

Movies like *The Graduate* in 1967 and *The Stepford Wives* in 1975 played on our anxieties about living in the suburbs. Mrs. Robinson, feeling trapped by the boredom and routine in her suburban life, desperately looked for meaning and excitement by seducing her daughter's boyfriend. And *The Stepford Wives* went a step beyond. Suddenly, the suburbs weren't just prisons for women; they were deadly. Malicious forces (husbands) were seeking to kill women and replace them with compliant sex robots. It was hardly a good advertisement for suburban living.

In fact, feminist-minded women lived in cities, not the 'burbs.

In *Welcome to the Dreamhouse*, Spigel discusses this phenomenon. She points to Mary Tyler Moore, or *That Girl's* Ann Marie. They lived in New York, not in the suburbs like Laura Van Dyke or Lucy Ricardo. In fact, at the beginning of *The Stepford Wives*, Joanna Eberhart, the main character, and her family are moving from the city to the suburbs. She is abandoning her job and life in the big city and already has misgivings about it, even before she finds out about the murders of independent-minded women in Stepford.

"A lot of the issues brought up in *The Stepford Wives* in 1975 are clearly unresolved today," says Spigel, who uses the film to discuss feminism in her classes at Northwestern. "Women still have to make really hard choices between careers and families. The Cosby family image of Clair Huxtable doing it all as an African-American woman is really not an option for most women of any color. It's really tiring and those choices are still really hard. For many women, and particularly poor women, it's still really difficult."

Desperate Housewives, then, could also be expressing fears and anxieties many of us already have of living in the suburbs. They are more dangerous than we thought, playing on many of our own fears of settling. Some women feel as if they might be losing something intangible by moving to the suburbs, by trading independence and perhaps their career for their family.

The same friends of mine who fretted about moving to the suburbs and missing the excitement of city life (great restaurants and shops just steps away) also have mixed feelings about becoming new moms. One kept her job in the city and deals with the added burden of a long early morning commute; the other has given up her job and stays at home in the 'burbs, almost completely divorced from city life. Both fret about whether or not they have made the right decision, and at the heart of their anxiety regarding their choices about motherhood is the move to the suburbs.

They fear not that their husbands will murder them and replace them with robots, but that they'll *become* robots all on their own—the sort of dowdy, out-of-touch soccer mom driving the minivan whose understanding of pop culture extends only to Elmo and SpongeBob SquarePants.

So perhaps the most desperate acts in *Desperate Housewives* aren't the overtly violent ones at all, but the subtle erosion of identity—the change of individual into wife, mother and suburbanite.

Desperate Housewives isn't just allowing us to live vicariously; it's giving our fears a new reality. The misgivings many of us feel about what we've given up by moving away from the city (or in some cases, never living in the city at all) now have shape and form. Murder in Suburbia might just be our hidden anxieties come to life. Wisteria Lane might just be the imaginary monster under our bed.

References

Beuka, Robert A. *SuburbiaNation: Reading Suburban Landscape in Twentieth-Century American Fiction and Film.* Palgrave Macmillan: 2004.

Spigel, Lynn. *Welcome to the Dreamhouse: Popular Media and Postwar Suburbs.* Duke University Press: 2001.

Cara Lockwood is the *USA Today* best-selling author of *I Do (But I Don't)*—which was made into a movie for Lifetime Television—*Pink Slip Party* and *Dixieland Sushi.* She lives in Chicago with her husband, where she is at work on her fourth novel. Visit her online at www.caralockwood. com.

Her friends say she's most like Susan, although she's not sure whether or not to take this as a compliment. She admits that she is a big klutz, but swears she's never locked herself out of her house in the nude.

Laura Caldwell

Girl Power Witty or Cat Fight City?

*With the rise of reality television has come a blurring of
the boundaries between truth and fiction, between what is
real and what is not. Our celebrities' home lives are followed more avidly than the movies or music for which they
originally attracted our attention: the subtext of Brad and
Angelina's relationship was far more interesting than their
filmed stint as Mr. and Mrs. Smith, and the movie's admittedly marginal success was fueled as much by the rumors
of their real-life love affair as by their on-screen chemis-
try. Is it any wonder, then, that our experience watching*
Desperate Housewives *could, like Laura Caldwell's, be
colored so thoroughly by our knowledge of what was happening behind the scenes?*

E ALL KNOW there's a fascination with "cat fights"—
quarrels, squabbles or all-out hair-pulling tussles between women. When *Desperate Housewives* first aired, I noticed the
character of Edie seemed to be cracking her knuckles and getting ready
for a little rumble-in-the-jungle with the neighbors. But as for the rest
of the ladies, once I peered through the hustle and high-jinks, what I
saw was, to steal a tired yet potent slogan from the Spice Girls, "Girl
Power."

Girl Power

I've always believed that girlfriends are the ticket to happiness and, at the risk of sounding too Deepak Chopra-ish, real personhood. Girlfriends are a mirror to your beauties and your failings. A good girlfriend can pinpoint both. (Example: "Honey, you *are* a good person. You're a wonderful wife and mother. You've totally got it together. Now you go change into two shoes that match, and I'll get little Tommy out of the liquor cabinet.") Yet a good girlfriend always makes you feel that your beauty far outweighs the failings. Girlfriends are our saviors.

Yet the fact is we don't live most of our moments with our girlfriends. Although TV shows like *Friends* would have you believe otherwise, the truth is we soldier on alone and then recap our escapades over the phone or a glass of wine. We spend most of our time with our co-workers, our kids and our husbands, but it's with our girlfriends that we dissect our lives; it's them we turn to for counseling.

With *Desperate Housewives*, I saw that kind of girlfriend reality. While these women were *very* different from each other (in a highly satirical, almost stereotyped kind of a way) and while they each had their own dramas, day-to-day grind and bouts of loneliness, they stood up for each other when duty called and they bonded when calamity hit.

This was evident in the first episode, in one of the few scenes with an alive-and-well Mary Alice. The women sat around a kitchen table and consoled Susan after her husband cheated on her. They tried to make her laugh, they traded dry comments about whether an erect penis had a conscience, but Susan felt comfortable enough to wonder, bleakly, how she would ever survive. Mary Alice told her to face her problems "head on."

When Mary Alice failed to take her own advice and instead took her own life, her girlfriends bonded together and embraced the task of cleaning out Mary Alice's closet, in order to spare her husband. They brought champagne and toasted "To Mary Alice. Good friend and neighbor. Wherever you are, we hope you've found peace."

The women of Wisteria Lane are also the mirror for each other. When Lynette's kids acted up at school, Bree didn't shirk from telling her, "Lynette, you are a great mother. But let's face it. Your kids are...a challenge." Lynette thanked her, saying, "That's the nicest way you could have said that" ("Who's That Woman?" 1–4).

In addition to the truthfully portrayed camaraderie of *Desperate Housewives*, the ladies of Wisteria Lane gave "Girl Power" new meaning for another reason as well—they struck a bizarre chord of recognition in women across America. Most female viewers, it seemed, didn't see themselves as one character or another; instead, they saw pieces of themselves in each of the characters. It was as if women everywhere were saying, *Yes, okay, fine. I admit it. I'm a little trampy, a little neurotic, a little bit harried, a little bit of a flake and a little bit of a sexpot. That's me, so what?* In addition to seeing women cover each other's backs on the show, there was strength in thinking that as a woman you no longer had to be one thing or another; that the days of defining ourselves too strictly were past us. The show seemed to bridge the gap between very different factions of women across the country.

The fact that most of the actresses in *Desperate Housewives* were all on the second, third or even fourth winds of their careers only helped matters. They had fought for these jobs. They embraced their roles, even if they didn't see themselves in the character they played. And like good girlfriends, we championed their comebacks.

Backstage Fireworks

As more became known about the talented cadre of *Desperate* women, the gossip started: They were all divas! They hated each other! But the PR machine cranked up the "good friends" angle, and for a while that was the official word. Celebrity magazines gushed about how the stars loved each other, how they were the best-est of buddies. On the show, the women protected each other, no matter their differences or prior squabbles, and it seemed to be true off-set, as well.

Then the *Vanity Fair* article came along. On the cover was a striking photograph of the *Desperate* stars in front of a glittering blue swimming pool, each wearing a brightly colored 1950s-style bathing suit. But only three of the stars were figured prominently. The other two—Marcia Cross and Felicity Huffman—were hidden inside the cover's foldout. The headline read: "Housewife Confidential: The Real-Life Soap Opera Behind TV's Hottest Show (You Wouldn't Believe What It Took Just To Get This Photo)."

Inside *Vanity Fair's* cover flap, the article was written like a suspense novel. Once upon a time there was a sleepy little town, and in that town, on a street called Wisteria Lane, something was rotten. Evil, some said. None of the residents would talk about the darkness that had befallen their ranks, but it was apparent, even to a lone visitor like a journalist, that everyone in town could smell it. *Who was the bad guy?* the reader of the article wondered. Who had brought the sinfulness to this otherwise idyllic burg? Every resident was a suspect, but eventually it became clear that the culprit was definitely one of the five beautiful women living there. The visitor to the town tried to root out the evil; he spoke to everyone, attempting to identify the one who'd shaken the beatific calm. But the ladies hushed anyone who tried to talk about the wickedness. (Reading the article, one quickly became exhausted from the sheer need to know *who-done-it*.) Finally, the visitor to the sleepy little town revealed that while all of the ladies have had their malevolent moments, Marcia Cross, who plays Bree on the show, was the root of the supposed evil. She couldn't stand Teri Hatcher, the article alleged. In fact, the dislike was so great she threw fits when Ms. Hatcher got any kind of special treatment and, in fact, had refused to be placed next to her at *Vanity Fair's* swimming-pool photo shoot.

The article, striking in its pettiness and sheer gossipy nature, was a letdown on other fronts, too. Where was the Girl Power? The camaraderie of the ladies? The bonding and the true-blue friendship? Was there some universal truth to the "cat fight" myth? Did women everywhere, famous or not, fight and bicker and backstab more often than men? And did *Desperate Housewives* foster the image of the strength, brilliance and beauty that could arise when women joined forces, or did the backstage turf wars of the *Desperate* cast wield a heavy blow to the image of women everywhere?

Cat Fight Mythology

There's no denying the curious fascination that surrounds women at each other's throats. Such allure was raised in the "Cat Fight" episode of *Seinfeld*, where the men salivated over the thought of Elaine in a scuffle with a co-worker with whom she didn't get along. Over and over, Elaine told the guys it *wasn't* a cat fight, but the idea was too delicious for anyone to take her seriously.

My conversations on this topic, with both men and women alike, seem to bolster the notion that women fight amongst themselves more frequently, and with more pettiness, than men. Men fight occasionally, many acknowledge, but the prevailing theory is that men simply duke it out and move on. Men scrap, and then the issue is dropped like a dirty diaper. But women, so the theory goes, let gripes fester; they gossip about the problem for a long time, sometimes years.

And yet there seems little interest in the topic of men quarreling. Instead our culture, particularly the media, loves a good buddy film where the male actors are touted to be buddies behind the camera as well. When *Ocean's Eleven* was released, the press trumpeted the friendship among the actors. Even if internal strife had broken out on the set, it's hard to imagine that there would ever have been a lead article in *Vanity Fair* about it. People simply aren't as mesmerized by the idea of a "dog fight."

Vanity Fair's article on *Desperate Housewives* was followed by repeats of the cat fight allegations in celebrity mags across the nation. The evilness backstage seemed to be growing with the wickedness of the show's plot. About that time, I began to sour slightly on the show. Don't get me wrong, I didn't stop watching. I wanted to see what in the hell was in that freaky toy chest just as much as the next girl, and who could turn off the tube when Gabrielle was about to spar with the hottie landscaper who loved her? Yet I didn't enjoy the show as much as I had before. I started noticing all the bickering during the show, and I was unable to shake all I'd heard about the backstage antics. I started wondering if *Desperate Housewives* was setting us back as women. It seemed that, early on, the show had been an ironic, exaggerated model of female diversity and bonding, but now both the show and the behind-the-scenes stories seemed to perpetuate the annoying myth that women really aren't friends, that they don't fight fair, that they hold grudges for all sorts of silly things.

Can Girl Power Rise Above the Fray?

Then came the series of episodes concerning Bree's husband's heart attack and eventual death. In one scene, Bree's friends on Wisteria Lane were at the hospital immediately after the attack, ignoring past tiffs. They held her hand, they comforted her, and when she told them to shut up or she would lose it, they did that, too. After Bree's husband passed away, the ladies joined her in front of her house, encouraging her to go ahead and fall apart. "Honey, you can let it out," Susan said ("Next," 2–1).

Although Bree didn't accept the offer to wail and rail to her friends, citing the fact that her mess of a mother-in-law was about to descend, these encounters reminded me of what I loved about *Desperate Housewives* in the first place—touching and yet realistic portrayals of Girl Power. Life is not a big *Friends* episode with hours spent by each other's sides, but we go running when a girlfriend is in crisis (whether a this-is-the-most-important-meeting-of-my-life-can-I-borrow-your-jacket kind of emergency or a my-husband-just-died type of disaster). When faced with tragedy, close female friends will bond together, and they are not afraid of emotions, even emotional meltdowns.

Maybe the crew of *Desperate Housewives* eventually realized the influence of "Girl Power"—both in their cast and audience—because as the second season prepared to launch, the tune changed. "This year, things are happier on the set of 'Housewives,'" read a headline from *USA Today*. The article went on to mention the "near-cat fighting" of the previous season, but claimed that the stars were more harmonious now. Still, the relations on Wisteria Lane were clearly not perfect. No less than five versions of a new *Desperate Housewives* advertisement had to be developed so that each star got the coveted center position.

Ultimately, whether there are backstage battles or not, the winner is the viewing public of *Desperate Housewives*. The show continues to portray a satirical, larger-than-life image of women the way they really are—sometimes gossipy, sometimes lonely, but always, always ready to go running when tragedy strikes. That's just what girlfriends do.

Laura Caldwell, who lives in Chicago with her husband, left a successful career as a trial attorney to become a novelist. She is the author of *Burning the Map, A Clean Slate, The Year of Living Famously, The Night I Got Lucky* and two novels of suspense, *Look Closely* and *The Rome Affair*. She is a contributing editor at *Lake Magazine* and an adjunct professor of law at Loyola University Chicago School of Law. Laura is frequently compared to Bree on *Desperate Housewives,* but she holds steadfast to the reasoning that this is only because of her red hair.

Julie Kenner

Sex and the Television Suburbs

Titillation has always been a key factor in Desperate Housewives' *marketing campaign; take, for example, Nicollette Sheridan's racy NFL locker-room spot. But is that the reason for* Desperate Housewives' *success? The way the show has pushed network television's sexual boundaries? Sex, they say, sells—but Julie Kenner isn't buying it.*

'VE FIGURED IT OUT. I know what makes the housewives desperate. It's not the suicide of their friend. It's not the hyperactivity of their children. It's not the pressure of keeping their houses looking like, well, a movie set. It's not even that their neighborhood is as filled with smoldering sexuality as it is with dangerous deceit.

It's that the women of Wisteria Lane have smashed their grocery carts and Aston Martins smack against a universal truth lurking right there on the Universal back lot: When it comes to television's representation of suburban moms and sexuality, the more things change, the more they stay the same.

Much of the hype and acclaim surrounding *Desperate Housewives* has focused on its cutting-edge nature. Words like "sharp" and "satirical" have been bandied about at least as much as "mega-hit" and "more commercial breaks than any other show on the air." But even more than style, the overarching gestalt of the show is sex. Or, rather, "Sex," the kind with a capital S. After all, wasn't it the suggestion of Sex that had advertisers pulling out after the famous Edie-in-the-locker-room commercial?

Not that sex is anything new in the world of television, but on Wisteria Lane, sex has been coupled with motherhood and Suburbia. Can it be so? Is Hollywood actually taking that giant leap and saying that suburban mommies can be sexy, too?

On the surface, the answer would certainly seem to be yes. After all, mere moments after the show hit the airwaves, the flurry of observations began—everything from serious academic analysis to *Cosmo*-like tips for using the Housewives as models for catching men. *See*, these commentators seemed to be saying, *look how sexy moms driving carpool and baking muffins can be.*

But is that really the message that *Desperate Housewives* delivers? Or is there, in fact, a subtle undertone tainting the veneer? A message that seems to have been embedded in television for decades, popping its head up once again in this icon of new-millennium feminism? A message that says that female sensuality, particularly among mothers, comes with a price not only above rubies, but above minivans and private school tuition as well?

A walk down memory lane (and Wisteria Lane, for that matter) illustrates the point. Wisteria Lane is the recycled incarnation of Colonial Drive on the Universal back lot, a street that has marked the location of an Animal House frat house and provided homes for the Munsters and the Cleavers, among other television families. It's appropriate that Wisteria Lane is recycled. Because so are the ultimate ideas regarding moms and sexuality espoused on the show.

Take the women from the black-and-white era. TV moms like Donna Reed and June Cleaver were idealized portrayals of women who stood by their men, vacuuming in pearls, and making sure that dinner was on the table and the kids' hands were washed. But while June Cleaver may be the quintessential television mom, she's not sexy, no matter how much of a thing you might have for heels, fitted waists and pearls.

June might have ruled the house (or at least the kitchen) and she'd certainly had the babies, but *sex* never factored into the equation. But June sprang from a different era, so surely the absence of all things sexual was simply a sign of the times. Right?

Maybe. But maybe not.

Case in point: Bree Van De Kamp. About as close to June Cleaver as a mom can come. But in this case, the show's cheerleaders would say, the perfect housekeeper also has a sex life. She's a sensual, sexual creature. Heck, she appeared in *Vanity Fair* in a bathing suit.

And she's a mom.

That's serious progress, right?

In theory, sure. But scratch that surface and the underlying picture isn't so pretty. Bree may be beautiful and sexy, but she's also unable to enjoy sex unless it's perfect. She's a control freak. Remember the burrito in Rex's hotel room? One thing out of place and sex is out of the question. In other words, she may be the June Cleaver of the bunch where housekeeping is concerned, but she has to pay for her organizational skills by being both cold and sexually dysfunctional.

Ultimately, while Bree may be fun to watch—causing women everywhere to thank Fate that we aren't burdened with Bree's issues—the overall message is neither a realistic portrayal of sexuality in the suburbs nor a positive representation from an allegorical standpoint. Bree's the woman in the show who values dinner around the table with her family. That "old-fashioned" value, however, has the misfortune of being associated with Bree's many, many neuroses.

And things don't get much better further down the street.

Springboard from the Cleaver and Van De Kamp homes across the San Fernando Valley to what is now called the Warner Brothers Ranch. Here we'll find another Americana neighborhood complete with plywood façades and a few functional interiors. We'll also find the home of Samantha and Darrin Stevens from *Bewitched*, another show that boasted an unrealistic picture of female sexuality.

Aired during a slightly different era from *Leave It To Beaver*, *Bewitched* managed to write such words as "groovy" and "hip" into its star's dialogue. Couple that with miniskirts and a few shimmies for good measure, and you might think that things had changed in the sexy TV mom department. After all, by the time the show was in color and miniskirts ruled the day, Samantha Stevens had a toddler. She was a soccer mom before such a creature even existed.

Trouble was, on those occasions when star Elizabeth Montgomery displayed a sexual nature, she was almost always playing the part of Serena, Samantha's wild and crazy cousin. As for mommy-Samantha, the extent of her sensuality tended toward a kiss and a martini.

Not exactly cutting edge.

Even so, Samantha had it better than the other moms with whom she crossed paths. Almost always, she was given the more flattering clothes and hairstyle. She was "the pretty one." The other moms tended to dress more frumpily.

Samantha's added value in the looks and sensuality department made sense. Not only was she the star of the show, but she had something that the other television moms didn't: She was a witch. And that meant that husband Darrin was playing with fire. How else to show that element of danger than to put her in attractive clothes, even though Larry Tate's wife ended up stuck in less-flattering outfits?

Decades later, Mom's sexuality must still be tempered in TV Land by the inevitable "something else," be it witchcraft or something completely different. Take Susan, arguably the star of *Desperate Housewives'* ensemble cast. Here we have a single mom who looks fabulous in jeans and T-shirts probably bought from The Limited, has a near-sisterlike relationship with her teenage daughter (who is ultimately more responsible than Mom) and dates the attractive plumber in the neighborhood. She's cute. She's sexy. She's over forty. She's self-employed (apparently gainfully, though we rarely actually see her working). And she's a mom.

Not too shabby as a role model for sexy suburban moms everywhere, eh?

Except that she's also the Klutz.

Because how can you be sexy *and* be a mom *and* be on television? Apparently, you can't now any more than you could decades ago.

If you're Samantha Stevens, your sex appeal is explained but also, more importantly, tempered by the fact that you're a witch (or else it's manifested in your sultry, swinging cousin). Susan doesn't need to have a slutty cousin, but she does have to be a klutz, a bit of a ditz and less mature than her fourteen-year-old daughter. In other words, she isn't really the mom. She's a big kid, too.

True, the sex appeal sometimes breaks through the klutziness, and we see Susan as an attractive adult instead of a big, awkward kid. But the fact that the device doesn't fully work doesn't change what it is—an unattractive or funny trait thrown in to tone down the sexuality of a television mom.

Where female sexuality plays a role in a television show, this concept of tempering that sensual nature with something else, be it klutziness or witchcraft or obsessive-compulsive disorder, has been a mainstay. Even supposedly "liberated" and "realistic" portrayals of women in television failed to include mothers who were sensual and sexy *and* free from sitcom-provided baggage.

In *Maude*, the title character—a woman divorced and remarried several times over—was comfortable with her sexuality. But she was also domineering and abrasive, a caricature of a liberal feminist whose sexuality was more of a platform than a personal characteristic.

As realistic women go, Norman Lear came closer to the mark with Ann Romano in *One Day at a Time*. A divorced mother of two teenage daughters trying to make a new life for herself as a single mom, Ann's situation and issues struck a realistic chord. But her sexuality, while acknowledged, was hardly a relevant part of the story.

One Day at a Time reflected a changing culture, highlighting women's shifting roles. On Wisteria Lane, Lynette does much the same. Our culture has seen a recent swing with regard to the role of women vis-à-vis work. In the days of June Cleaver, a woman's work was at home. In the *Maude* years, women were "empowered" and encouraged (often to the point of derision if they resisted) to join the workforce, standing toe-to-toe with men. In the last few years, however, many professional women have left the boardroom for the playroom, choosing to stay home with their children. And when viewers first met Lynette that was the choice she had made. As a former executive turned stay-at-home mom, with four children under the age of six, Lynette epitomized the harried housewife. The changing mores of society were further reflected in season two, when Lynette went back to work and her husband remained at home with the kids.

Interestingly, while the character of Lynette comes across as significantly less sexy (except, of course, in photo ops for the show itself), her sex life is expressed in a far more realistic fashion. Lynette and her husband are still wildly attracted to each other, so much so that Lynette once had to put the brakes on her husband's amour (with a well-placed right hook) simply to make sure four kids didn't become five in nine months (or whatever the gestation period on television might be). Certainly that's a step up from the "no sex please" attitude of Debra on *Everybody Loves Raymond*. A wonderful show, to be sure, but a running shtick centered around Debra's definite lack of interest in sex, drawing humor from the fact that Ray wasn't getting any.

But while Lynette certainly has sex (as do all the Housewives, and as June Cleaver must have in order to end up with Wally and the Beav), her sexuality is once again tempered. Her trysts with her husband are often fast and furious, with Lynette clad in sweats and baby spit. Realistic? Probably. But compare that with her portrayal in season two. Once Lynette rejoined the workforce, suddenly the viewer was treated to an image of Lynette as the Siren. Her provocative dance in the bar may not have been designed to catch her a man, but it did show Lynette off in a more sensual light. And consider why she did it: She was trying to avoid going out at night with her boss, who believed that being a happily married mother meant Lynette wasn't competition. To do so, Lynette changed her entire persona—being sexy meant becoming something else, a person she wasn't on a day-to-day basis with her husband or family. She couldn't be both a mother *and* sexy enough to present a threat to her young, single boss.

That's not to say there haven't been Sirens who were also moms over the course of television history. Of course there have. But for the most part, television moms who are overtly sexual are also overtly dysfunctional. Peg, for example, on *Married with Children*: Here was a woman who wasn't afraid to admit that she wanted sex, but was the butt of the joke (along with her husband) because of it.

It's interesting to note that the two Housewives who are "allowed" to flaunt their sexuality are the two who are not moms—Gabrielle and Edie. Even they, however, have a price to pay.

Gabrielle is cast as the gold digger. She's beautiful and sexy and she knows it. She's also unhappy, unfaithful and trapped, both in her marriage and, briefly, with an unwanted pregnancy. In other words, she's paying the price for her sexuality.

The neighborhood's most infamous single gal, Edie, is surely the most overtly sexual. She makes no apologies for wanting to snag the eligible men in the neighborhood, and because of it she's portrayed as a competitive backstabber. She exudes a raw, blatant sexuality and confidence. And yet, once again, that display of feminine sensuality is tempered by her inability to bond with the Housewives. She's the outsider, the slut. Instead of being empowered, she's pitied. Again, Edie is paying the price for her sexuality.

For a show that's so often hailed as cutting edge, the underlying message with regard to sexuality is hardly forward-thinking. And yet still the show draws a huge audience consisting primarily of women, myself included. We tune in for the glamour and the plot and the mystery and the overall soap opera aspects of the show. Not because the show is a bastion of realism. We tune in because we know that the Housewives *aren't* real. They're carefully crafted archetypes designed to entertain.

The Oxford English Dictionary defines an archetype as "the original pattern or model...an ideal pattern." In actual fact, though, the women of Wisteria Lane aren't really the "ideal" anything, and most especially not in terms of the sexuality of the suburban soccer mom. Truth be told, these women are a mess. Why then, do we care so much? ("We" being used loosely, as in "me, the loyal viewer who never misses an episode and has TiVo programmed, just in case.") We're talking entertainment here, folks. And to that end, *Desperate Housewives* succeeds in spades.

The Wisteria Lane women exist in a world of labels and cubbyholes. They're bits and pieces. No one can doubt who the Stepford wife on the Lane is. Or the harried mom. Or the earnest single mother. But these characters compel us for two key reasons: First, because of those cubbyholes—because they remain true to the labels even while transcending them. Second, and possibly more important, because the flawed nature of the characters represents a universal truth: No woman really can "do it all." The fantasy of a supermom who can effortlessly juggle work, kids, relationships, housekeeping and a sex life is just that—a fantasy. In revealing that, frankly and with compassion, the show has made great gains on its primetime predecessors.

And while the show may put a price on the sexuality of the housewives, at least they *have* a sex life. For the most part, they enjoy and embrace their sexuality despite their mommy status and the fact that they're over forty. In the world of television, which tends to cater to a much younger set, that's a rare thing, and it reflects the changing demographics of the audience.

The Housewives also represent the power center of the show. And, just like the price that comes with a television female's sexuality, women holding the power in the television family is hardly a new concept. It's almost as if that's the trade-off: By sacrificing the realistic portrayal of female sexuality, shows are allowed to push the envelope by flipping the stereotypical family power structure.

Take *I Dream of Jeannie*. Can anyone doubt who was really in charge there? Or *Bewitched*? And, lest we think it's only magical women who wield the power, look at the moms in *The Partridge Family, Happy Days, Married With Children, The Cosby Show, Roseanne, Everybody Loves Raymond*, even *The Munsters*. It wasn't always overt, but there was no doubt who really ran those families. Just as there's no doubt where the power lies in the world of *Desperate Housewives*. Sure the men on Wisteria Lane get a few good tugs in now and then, but ultimately, it's all about the women. And that's true even though there's not a "superwoman" among them.

The bottom line? The women of Wisteria Lane are of the kind that have been peppering television for decades. But what works so well about *Desperate Housewives* is the way the writers have taken those old archetypes and infused them with wit and warmth, not to mention secrets and mysteries.

Which is why fans tune in each week. Not because the show is cutting edge. It's not. But on a Sunday night—before the workweek begins, before the kids pile into the minivan—an hour of pure entertainment is good enough for me.

Julie Kenner's first book hit the stores in February of 2000, and she's been on the go ever since. A national best-selling author, Julie is also a former RITA finalist, the winner of *Romantic Times'* Reviewer's Choice Award for Best Contemporary Paranormal of 2001, and winner of the Reviewers International Organization's award for best romantic suspense of 2004. In addition to romance and paranormal women's fiction, she writes chick-lit suspense (her current "Game" series includes the releases *The Givenchy Code* and *The Manolo Matrix*). Her 2005 release, *Carpe Demon: Adventures of a Demon-Hunting Soccer Mom*, was selected as a Booksense Summer Pick, was a Target Breakout Book, was a Barnes & Noble bestseller and is in development as a feature film with Warner Brothers and 1492 Pictures. Look for the sequel, *California Demon*, in 2006. A former attorney who now works at home and has a three-year-old daughter, Julie figures she's got a little bit of both Lynette and Susan in her blood. Visit Julie on the Web at www.juliekenner.com.

Lani Diane Rich

Why the Best Nighttime Soap Ever Is *Not* a Nighttime Soap. Damnit.

Don't call Lani Diane Rich's favorite Sunday night television a soap opera. It's not that soap operas are bad; it's that their writing is. And while there are some things, as Julie Kenner demonstrated, that you can criticize Desperate Housewives *for, the quality of its writing isn't one of them.*

I REMEMBER THE EXACT MOMENT I fell in love with *Desperate Housewives*. It was a late Sunday night. I'd finally gotten the kids to bed and switched on the television to see Lynette sitting on a soccer field in the midst of a Ritalin-withdrawal-inspired nervous breakdown. Susan and Bree had found her and were sitting with her, listening to her sob over her inadequacy as a mother. They shared their experiences of motherhood—the weeping, the fear, the frustration. To my surprise, I found myself weeping along with them.

This moment resonated with me so deeply because I'd had a very similar experience—minus the Ritalin addiction. My youngest daughter, age two at the time, had been up all night reminding me why I have such a strong aversion to vomit, and my oldest daughter was pulling the four-year-old-with-attitude bit, and all I wanted in the world was some Children's Tylenol. My younger daughter was crying and my older daughter was whining and I finally yelled, "Shut up for a minute!" just as a woman with two small boys in her cart was walking by. She gave

59

me this look, a combination of pity and loathing, and then she smiled at my four-year-old as if to say, "I'll be praying for you, dear." And I wanted to smack her. Hard. How dare she judge me? How dare she pity my child? I'm a good mother. I love my kids. I'm funny. I can't cook worth a damn, but everyone has weaknesses. Rather than confronting the woman, though, I simply continued my fruitless search for the Children's Tylenol. A clerk asked if she could help, and I asked her where on God's green earth they kept the Children's Tylenol, and she pointed it out—right in front of me. I wept as I waited in line, I wept on the drive home, and I wept during naptime and well into the night. I was certain I was the only mother in the world who felt that incompetent, who was that desperate just to find a way to make it through the day.

Two years later, I watched Lynette slump next to a goalpost and weep as her girlfriends rallied around her, and I realized *Desperate Housewives* was not just another campy, cheesy, guilty-pleasure television show. This was something special; these were my people.

I was, at first, a tad alarmed that I'd found my people in a nighttime soap, because nighttime soap people are not my people. They're not anyone's people. They're Alexis and Krystle and Billy and Amanda. They have cat fights in swimming pools. They blow up entire apartment complexes. They fake pregnancies only to find out they really are pregnant and the man they tricked into marrying them is not the father and then, just before the critical moment when the actress is supposed to start getting fat, the character loses the pregnancy and discovers she has ovarian cancer. That's the deal with nighttime soaps; they're unreal, and they're fun to watch *because* they're so unreal.

But *Desperate Housewives* is different. It combines the real with the unreal, contrasts the perfect with the flawed. And yeah, admittedly, there's stuff in there that stretches the suspension of disbelief (the second season's clanging basement prisoner comes to mind), but it's not solely the outrageous storylines that make a nighttime soap a nighttime soap.

It's the writing.

It's the bad, bad, *bad* writing.

Now, this is not to say that the people who write for nighttime soaps are necessarily bad *writers*. Nighttime soaps are supposed to have bad writing. That's what nighttime soaps are—wild hair, snazzy outfits, outrageous scenarios and bad, bad, *bad* writing. Trite dialogue. Unbelievable characters. It's what makes the clocks on Melrose Place tick.

Now, I'll grant you, *Desperate Housewives* definitely has the hair, outfits and outrageous scenarios down pat. But the writing is not simply *not bad.* It's excellent, far too good for this Sunday night gem to be labeled as a nighttime soap. So, in the interests of ending this unfair practice—and, you know, amusing myself—here are my reasons why the writing on *Desperate Housewives* is far too fabulous for the show to be classified as a nighttime soap:

1. Mrs. Solis and John, the Teenage Gardener

I know, it sounds like a really bad erotica story, but here's the thing—a storyline which, in and of itself, just reeks of nighttime soap is actually a love story with quite a bit of depth. On the surface, the story is pure cheddar: A shallow, neglected trophy wife takes up with the sizzle-hot teenage domestic staff. Yawn. But from the moment Gabrielle's young stud first called her "Mrs. Solis"—which he did consistently throughout the span of the relationship—you knew there was something different going on here. It also spawned some of *Desperate Housewives'* best scenes: John jumping out the window and waving to Carlos as he trimmed the hedges, sans pants; Gabrielle running home from a social event to mow the lawn in her gown so Carlos didn't fire John for neglecting his duties; John's mother attacking Susan's dress at the charity fashion show after she deduced that a housewife was sleeping with her son but assumed it was the wrong one. But even with all the fun moments, these cheesy waters ran amazingly deep. When Gabrielle talked to the priest about her understanding of what it is to be a good person, her experience as a beautiful trophy wife looking for affection rang startlingly true. Gabrielle's understanding of her own shallowness gives her depth. One of the most touching moments was when Gabrielle told John she didn't love him so that he would go away to college and make more of himself. Although Gabrielle's moments of depth are few and far between, in the first season they created an engaging and revealing storyline in the one place you'd never expect to find it.

2. Too-Stupid-To-Live Susan

Susan. Susan, Susan, *Susan.* Here is a woman who accidentally burned down her neighbor's house, got herself locked out of her house naked, put dog food on her face to make a dog like her, then nearly killed the mutt when he swallowed her big floppy earring. But number one on the Stupid Susan Hit Parade? Mike.

Now, I like Mike as much as the next girl. As a matter of fact, I lurrrrrrrrrve Mike. (And James Denton. But that's another essay entirely.) Here, we're talking about Susan making with the stupid. She got a crush on Mike the Plumber and threw herself at him. She showed up at his house, dressed up for a hot date, and found another woman there. She followed him to a dive bar, and got hit in the face with a mechanical bull. Without demanding much by the way of an explanation from Mike, she decided to trust him and give it a shot. Then one day while looking for dog biscuits in his house, she found wads of cash and a gun in his cabinet. Instead of asking him directly, she snooped around his house and fell through his bathroom floor. He caught her snooping, got mad and threw her out, and when he recanted and came to her, telling her she could ask him anything, she didn't ask him *why in the world a plumber needs wads of cash and a gun*; she slept with him. Hmmm. On their Valentine's Day date he collapsed due to a gunshot wound that he told her was self-inflicted, and even after hearing the hospital staff say the story was crap, she believed him. No questions. Then, when she discovered he'd killed a cop and dealt drugs, she had the nerve to be surprised. Now, as it turns out, Mike's an okay guy, but he could have been the Serial Killer of the Year, and Susan still would have pursued the relationship. Because Susan? Is stupid.

And yet...I can't help but love Susan. I love her for her good intentions, I love her for her great kid, I love her for the fact that she gets to sleep with Mike and hence I get to (vicariously, *fine*) sleep with Mike. I love the fact that she lives life vulnerably, the way most of us are too afraid to. Yes, at times she's dumber than a box of rocks, but she's also one of the bravest characters on television. She does and says what most of us would only think about doing and saying, and it's not because she's too stupid to understand that it involves risk, but because she's courageous enough to accept that risk. She feels everything fully, completely, and she never shuts down or gets bitter—not for long, anyway. She manages to live through difficult times and still experience life with a full heart. It takes very smart writing to create a character this dumb and still make her this incredibly lovable.

3. Lynette and Her Kids

As a woman who left the full-time workforce to raise her kids, I probably over-relate to Lynette's storyline, but I think this is one of the most brilliantly and bravely written storylines in television today. For as long as I can remember, mothers have been portrayed in one of three ways on television:

- the happy, cake-baking, diorama-building Donna Reed-y type
- the professional woman who still manages to get in some super-quality time with her precocious tots
- Mommie Dearest

This, as I discovered, is not entirely accurate. Some days are Donna Reed days, and some days are Mommie Dearest days, and the line between them is very fine indeed. I'll admit, Lynette's kids are very close to caricatures, the common uncontrollable brats that exist solely for the comedy value and then disappear when the writers want to make room for the adult storylines. But her kids become special not in and of themselves, but in the fact that they, like real kids, don't disappear out of convenience. Especially in the first season, Lynette never played a scene in which her kids were not a factor. They are appendages, they are part of her, and that is motherhood. It's nothing short of a miracle that Marc Cherry was able to understand this without having experienced motherhood firsthand (which, I'm assuming, since he's a guy, he hasn't). Lynette's struggle to be a good mother and a complete person unto herself at the same time is played for comedy one moment and pathos the next. I cried with her when she sat, crumpled and defeated, on that soccer field. When Susan and Bree shared their motherhood horror stories and Lynette wailed, "We should tell each other this stuff," she was right. And through the miracle of really good writing, Marc Cherry and his staff did just that. And for that, I now have a big fat crush on Marc Cherry. He's gay, I'm married, I don't care. I love me my Marc Cherry.

4. Bree and Rex: Now You Hate Them, Now You Don't

When I first saw Bree, despite the fact that Marcia Cross plays that character within an inch of her fictional life, I didn't like her. She's That Woman, the perfect wife and mother that makes the rest of us feel inadequate even on our good days. Her yard is perfect, her hair obeys out of sheer terror, her figure is flawless and her smile relentless. Not to mention she's uptight, she's judgmental, she gave a grieving widower a basket of muffins and insisted *she'd need the basket back* and she announced to an entire dinner party that Rex cried when he ejaculated. Rex, for his share of the blame, was a big knobhead. He degraded his wife in front of their therapist, he demanded she feed him in high style while he was moving out of the house, he bribed the kids into taking his side in the divorce and he publicly humiliated her by cheating with the local high-society hooker. Rex was like the bad aftertaste you get after chewing chalky antacid tablets. *Phbbbbbattt.*

And yet... and yet. Somehow, by injecting little moments of quiet humanity into each of them, by the end of the first season, I really loved them both. When Bree shared her imperfect motherhood moments with Lynette, I softened toward her. When she leaned lovingly over Rex's hospital bed after discovering his infidelity and whispered, in no uncertain terms, that she was going to make him pay through the nose for all the pain he'd caused her, I cheered for her. By the time she told Gabrielle that "good friends offer to help in a crisis; great friends don't take no for an answer," I was fully in love with Bree.

As for Rex, the moments were more subtle, yet just as endearing. When he revealed that he gave the kids the gifts so that they'd stay with Bree, I rolled my eyes and accepted it. When, in the bedroom with Maisy Gibbons, he admitted that he couldn't ask Bree to fulfill his sexual fantasies because he cared if she rejected him, I believed it. And after the heart attack, when he came running back to Bree and I wanted to hate him because he was a sniveling whiner who got his mid-life crisis square in the chest and now wanted Mommy to take care of him... I didn't. When he sat down at the table with the divorce lawyers and told Bree he didn't want the divorce, he took his lumps when she kept going, and I respected that. He was sincere when he told her that he wanted her back, and that he was sorry, and I accepted it. It wasn't until he was an elitist butthole to George the Creepy Pharmacist and I instantly forgave him because, well, George was creepy, that I realized I'd grown to love him, too. Not because the writers demanded that I love him, but because they made him lovable. They made him earn his way back. Out of two characters that were on the surface wholly unlikable, these writers created fully formed people steeped in their own fallibility, and it made them somehow, miraculously, lovable. It was nothing short of brilliant.

5. The Mystery

From the moment Paul dug up the toy chest out of the pool floor, I was hooked. The story snaked around the ankles of everyone on Wisteria Lane, both main characters and supporting, but it always came back to Mary Alice and the suicide shot heard round the world. Why would a woman with a seemingly perfect life end it like that? From Zach's confession that he'd killed his sister to Paul whacking Martha Huber with a blender, the story escalated from week to week into a final note that was well earned and satisfying. With the exception of the season-ending cliffhanger—which screamed nighttime soap and was way below this writing staff—the story was perfect. Even in retrospect, as I watch the episodes again, the story holds up. That's no easy task, and it's definitely a sign of great writing.

6. Secondary Characters

Martha Huber. Felicia Tilman. Karen McClusky. Maisy Gibbons. While the casting department deserves almost as much credit for these characters as the writers (Christine Estabrook! Harriet Sansom Harris! Kathryn Joosten! Sharon Lawrence! It's like I've died and gone to character actor heaven), it's still the writers that created these little jewels of characterization to sparkle in the background. From Martha Huber's money problems to Karen McClusky's lost son, the first season gave us a plethora of tiny little moments that were completely owned by these characters, and in those moments, we loved them as much as we did the main characters.

7. Dialogue, Dialogue, Dialogue

I'm about to confess something. I don't care how good the story is, if the dialogue is bad, I'm outta there. Luckily, this is not a problem with *Desperate Housewives*. While the storylines are fun and intriguing, in the end it's the dialogue that keeps me coming back. In a world where a man can say to his wife, "I'm sick of the bizarre way your hair doesn't move," you know there's gonna be some good zingers. So here we go with the First (and probably only) Annual (although don't look for it next year) *Desperate Housewives* Best Dialogue Awards, giving credit where credit is due: to the writers.

Best Zinger: Marc Cherry, for this line from Rex ("Pilot," 1–1)

> REX: You're this plastic suburban housewife with her pearls and her spatula who says things like, "We owe the Hendersons a dinner."

Best Candid Sex Talk: Tracey Stern, for Bree's candid sex discussion with Dr. Goldfine ("Running to Stand Still," 1–6)

> BREE: The only thing I don't like about sex is the scrotum. I mean, obviously it has its practical applications, but I'm just not a fan.

Best "Oh, No He Di-in't": Oliver Goldstick, for this interaction between Karl and Susan, wherein Karl tries to justify his philandering ("Pretty Little Picture," 1–3)

KARL: I don't know what to say, Susan. The heart wants what it wants.
SUSAN: What's that mean?
KARL: I fell in love.
SUSAN: While you were married to someone else!
KARL: The heart wants what it wants.

Best Catty-But-True Remark: Marc Cherry, for Martha Huber's response to Edie's refusal to wear donated clothing after her house burns down ("Ah, But Underneath," 1–2)

MARTHA: Edie, you can be homeless or you can be ungracious. You really can't afford to be both.

Best "Yep, That's Exactly How It Would Play In My Marriage": David Schulner, for this Lynette and Tom moment, played while on the escalator at the mall ("Move On," 1–11)

LYNETTE: The only reason you made love to me the other night is because you'd just seen Claire naked.
TOM: Wha—? Oh, crap.

Best Six-Words-Says-It-All Moment: Kevin Etten, for John the Gardener's heartfelt yet obviously misguided proposal ("Your Fault," 1–13)

JOHN: Mrs. Solis? Will you marry me?

Best "I'm Gonna Have To Use That Line Someday": Tom Spezialy, for the moment Lynette threatens to whup her kleptomaniacal kids ("Love Is in the Air," 1–14)

LYNETTE: Time to pick your poison. How 'bout a belt? It's a classic. Well, we could go with the old hickory stick. It's a cliché, but it's pretty effective. I know, we'll go with the spatula. The holes give it less wind resistance. Moves faster.

Best "You Can Say That Again": Alexandra Cunningham, for this moment after Susan breaks up with Mike for forgetting to mention he'd once killed a man ("The Ladies Who Lunch," 1–16)

MIKE: You can't believe I'm some cold-blooded killer.
SUSAN: No, of course I don't believe that. But I also didn't believe that Karl was going to cheat on me and I didn't believe Mary Alice was going to kill herself. I mean, let's face it, Mike. Blind faith is not my friend.

As you can see from these examples, great dialogue is what takes good writing and makes it something truly special. Without these taut one-liners and verbal volleys, *Desperate Housewives* wouldn't be anywhere near as good as it is. Rule of thumb: If you're wishing you'd said it yourself, that's great dialogue.

Verdict: No Nighttime Soap

So, there you have it: Tight plots, great dialogue, characterization you can bounce a quarter off of and a strict adherence to the school of Let's-Not-Take-Ourselves-Too-Seriously. What Marc Cherry and his writers have done is create a guilty-pleasure show that no one should feel guilty about enjoying. So hold your head up high as you clear your schedule for Sunday nights. *Desperate Housewives* is not a nighttime soap; it's all of us, broken down to our very essence (and perhaps genetically enhanced a bit), and then presented back to us for our viewing pleasure.
And oh, what a pleasure it is. . . .

Lani Diane Rich is an author, college instructor, mother of two and... something else, but she can't remember. She lives in Syracuse, New York, where she writes really fun novels which she hopes you will go out and buy immediately, because Cheerios ain't cheap. You can find her at www.lanidianerich.com.
And if she were a Desperate Housewife, she'd totally be Lynette.

Will the Real Bree Van De Kamp Please Stand Up?

Bree Van De Kamp is easily the hardest Housewife to pin down. Is she a doormat or a dominatrix? A loving wife or a vengeful harpy? Think you know? Take a seat on Whitney Gaskell's panel, and try your luck.

HE TELEVISION GAME SHOW *Which One Is It?* is filmed in a large, cold studio, now buzzing with activity. The game show, which has been on the air for decades, has seen its ratings wane in recent years, and yet today nearly every seat in the studio audience is filled with fans, lookie-loos and tourists who snatched up the free tickets that an intern handed out on the street.

The stars of the show—a panel of three men and one women, all semi-famous but on the downside slope of their careers—sit behind a table on the left side of the shoddy set. The show's sign, painted gold and lit up with blinking lights, hangs over their heads. A glittering silver curtain that looks like it was knitted out of Christmas tree tinsel hangs to the right of the stage. The intro music begins to blare loudly, and, when prompted by a flashing yellow light, the audience applauds.

The Host runs on to the stage, grinning widely and waving at the audience. They applaud even louder.

"Thank you, ladies and gentlemen! Welcome to *Which One Is It?*" the Host announces as he takes his place behind the lectern at the center of the stage. "The game show about finding out who the *real* contestant is. The rules on *Which One Is It?* are simple: We introduce a contestant and two imposters who are just pretending to be the contestant. Our panel asks them all questions, while they try to figure out...*Which One Is It?!*"

The studio audience shouts out the name of the show along with the host, and he rewards them with an even larger smile. The Host recently paid eight thousand dollars for porcelain veneers, and he likes to show them off whenever possible.

"First let me introduce our panel," the Host says with a flourish of his hand. "Best known for his role as the imposing Dr. Knightly on the hit medical show *Resuscitate*, our very own Charles Montigue!"

The camera pans to a dour, bald man with a full beard. He glares into the camera as the audience applauds politely.

"The writer of the weekly syndicated column *I Know Better Than You*, Patricia Rose!"

More applause. Patricia Rose smiles and waggles her fingers.

"Stand-up comedian and one of the funniest men alive, Billy Zips!"

Billy holds up his hand like a gun, and pretends to shoot the camera. He winks and grins.

"And finally, you knew him as Ted Tucson on the soap opera *Another Day In Paradise*...please give a warm welcome to Fred Sanderson."

Fred beams, and waves. The audience continues to clap, although they seem to be losing their enthusiasm.

"Now, let's play *Which One Is It?!* Our contestant today is Bree Van De Kamp," the Host says.

The silver curtain lifts up, revealing three wide-screen television sets. A picture of a woman—the same woman—is frozen on each screen. Her shoulder-length auburn red hair has been blown out to a glossy sleekness, the ends curling up coyly. She's wearing a lavender twin set over a gray wool skirt, and a strand of pearls hangs at her throat. Her features are elegant and refined: the greenish-blue eyes are wide and clear, the lips are curved in a bemused smile, the perfectly tweezed eyebrows rise up at sardonic angles.

"Is this supposed to be a joke?" Charles wheezes. He is the oldest panelist, and is devoid of humor.

"When they said there were going to be cutbacks on the show, I didn't realize they were going to get rid of the contestants," Billy quips. The comedian has an impish face, with deep dimples and twinkling blue eyes. "If they wanted to save a few pennies they should have just fired Charles."

"A very few pennies, indeed," Charles grumps.

"I better lay off the lunchtime martinis...I'm not seeing double, I'm seeing triple," Patricia says with a brassy laugh. She's top heavy, and wears her hair piled high on her head, lacquered in place with hairspray.

"Take a look at those legs," Fred leers. He has an orange tan, wears a bad toupee and is rumored to be gay. He compensates by making a point of ogling every attractive woman that appears on the show.

"Which ones?" Patricia wisecracks.

"Any of them. All of them. As long as they're not yours," Fred replies. He and Patricia loathe one another. He suspects—correctly—that she's the one who floated the rumor to the tabloids about his being gay.

The Host's smile slips a bit. He doesn't like it when the panelists step on his lines.

"Now, now. I haven't finished introducing today's contestant," he chides them. There is an edge to his voice, although when he turns back toward the audience, his smile is gamely in place. "Bree Van De Kamp is married to Dr. Rex Van De Kamp, and she's a stay-at-home-mother to her two teenage children, son Andrew and daughter Danielle. Her interests include cooking, gardening, sewing and upholstery."

"Yes, but where is she?" Billy asks. He makes a big show of looking under the panel's table, as if the producers might have stashed her there. The audience laughs appreciatively, and Billy winks at them.

"On today's show, we're going to try something a little different," the Host says.

"You don't say," Charles says dryly.

"Instead of a live contestant, today we're going to play three sets of clips. Each montage will show a very different side of Bree Van De Kamp. We'll then leave it up to our distinguished panel," the Host pauses to smirk at the idea that the panel is anything other than a group of washed-up has-beens clinging to their tattered scraps of fame, "to see if they can determine which one is the real Bree."

The panel looks at him blankly.

"I don't get it," Fred says.

"What a surprise," Patricia says, rolling her eyes.

"You're going to play clips that are all of the same woman? What's for us to figure out?" Billy asks. "Who are we going to question?"

"You're not going to question anyone. You're just going to guess which set of clips shows the essence of the real Bree Van De Kamp," the Host explains. He flashes a wide, toothy smile.

"So, these aren't three different woman who all just look alike? They aren't triplets?" Fred asks.

"No! The clips all show the same woman," the Host says. He's losing patience. "Look, just watch. Here's Bree Number One."

The Host holds up a remote control, and hits a play button. The image of Bree Van De Kamp on the first television springs to life.

The first clip shows Bree, accompanied by her family, approaching Paul Young after his wife's funeral. She's dressed immaculately, and is carrying baskets brimming with baked goods.

> PAUL: Bree, you shouldn't have gone to all this trouble.
> BREE: It was no trouble at all. Now the basket with the red ribbon is filled with desserts for your guests. But the one with the blue ribbon is just for you and Zachary. It's got rolls, muffins, breakfast type things.
> PAUL: Thank you.
> BREE: Well, the least I could do is make sure you boys had a decent meal to look forward to in the morning. I know you're out of your minds with grief.
> PAUL: Yes, we are.
> BREE: Of course, I will need the baskets back once you're done. ("Pilot," 1–1)

The next clip shows the Van De Kamps sitting around the table in their formal dining room. Candles twinkle and the silver gleams, and it's obvious a tremendous amount of energy has gone into preparing the meal. Looking disgruntled, Bree's family stares down at their soup bowls.

> DANIELLE: Why can't we ever have normal soup?
> BREE: Danielle, there is nothing abnormal about basil puree.
> DANIELLE: Just once, can we have a soup that people have heard of? Like, french onion or navy bean.
> BREE: First of all, your father can't eat onions, he's deathly allergic. And I won't even dignify your navy bean suggestion. So. How's the osso bucco? ("Pilot," 1–1)

In the final clip, Bree and Rex are sitting side by side in the office of Dr. Goldfine, a marriage therapist.

> BREE: And so, there's just the four of us. My oldest son Andrew is sixteen, Danielle is fifteen, and...

(BREE reaches into her purse for photographs of the children.)

GOLDFINE: I don't need to see pictures. Bree, you've spent most of the hour engaging in small talk.

BREE: Oh, have I?

GOLDFINE: Yes. Rex has been very vocal about his issues. Don't you want to discuss your feelings about your marriage?

BREE: Um. . . .

REX: This is the thing you gotta know about Bree. She doesn't like to talk about her feelings. To be honest, it's hard to know if she has any. Does she feel anger, rage, ecstasy? Who knows? She's always . . . pleasant. And I can't tell you how annoying that is. Whatever she feels is so far below the surface that . . . that no one can see . . . she uses all those domestic things. . . .

(BREE, meanwhile, has stopped listening to REX. Instead, she's fixated on a loose button on DR. GOLDFINE's jacket. She again reaches into her purse, this time extracting a sewing kit.)

GOLDFINE: Bree? Bree.

BREE: I'm sorry?

GOLDFINE: Would you like to respond to what Rex just said?

BREE: Oh, um. . . .

GOLDFINE: Is there some truth there? Do you use housework as a way to disengage emotionally?

BREE: Of course not.

(BREE quickly drops the sewing kit back into her purse.) ("Ah, But Underneath," 1–2)

The video stops and then switches back to the same picture of Bree that's frozen on the other two television screens. The studio audience claps politely.

"A model wife," Charles says sagely.

"Oh, please. She's a Stepford Wife," Patricia says. "She's plastic."

"I disagree. She cooks, sews, takes care of her family. She's everything you'd want from a wife," Charles says. He looks surprised when the women in the audience boo him.

"Thank you, ladies," Patricia says, nodding and grinning. She claps appreciatively. "You tell him."

"She may be plastic, but she's smokin' hot," Fred announces. "I wouldn't kick her out of bed for eating crackers."

"You have a better chance of building a rocket out of Tinkertoys and flying to the moon than you would of getting together with that woman," Billy says. Patricia guffaws appreciatively and Fred looks annoyed.

"It's unfortunate that the domestic arts previous generations of mothers and wives excelled in have been lost in this age of fast food and sitcoms," Charles says, to which the audience boos even louder. Charles crosses his arms and looks disgusted.

"I was trained as a classical actor. I played Hamlet! And this is where I end up," he mutters. "A tacky game show, surrounded by a cast of untalented louts."

"Now, now," the Host says, looking startled. "Let's move on to the next set of clips. Here's Bree Number Two."

The Host clicks his remote control again, and this time the middle television springs into action. In the first clip, Bree and Rex are in a seedy hotel room. Bree is standing in front of Rex in a full-length mink coat. Suddenly, she drops the coat, revealing that underneath all she has on is a lacey red bra and matching panties.

REX: You look amazing.
BREE: Thanks. I was hoping you'd notice. ("Running to Stand Still," 1–6)

In the next clip, Bree is in a restaurant eating lunch with Dr. Goldfine. She looks as prim and cheerful as always, and the doctor has a pained expression on his face. "I love sex. I love everything about it: the sensations, the smells," Bree says, to the doctor's chagrin. "I especially love the feel of a man. All that muscle and sinew pressed against my body. And then when you add friction. Mmm. The tactile sensation of running my tongue over a man's nipple ever so gently. And then there's the act itself; two bodies becoming one in that final eruption of pleasure. To be honest, the only thing I don't like about sex is the scrotum. I mean, obviously it has its practical applications, but I'm just not a fan" ("Running to Stand Still," 1–6).

The next clip shows Bree and Rex sitting together on a couch, watching a domination porn movie. Rex looks vaguely uncomfortable, while Bree is openly shocked.

BREE: What the hell did your mother do to you?
REX: What?
BREE: Well, come on, this just reeks of unresolved childhood trauma.
REX: This has nothing to do with my mother, Bree, this is a preference.

Bree: It's a perversion.

Rex: For God's sake, you promised to be supportive.

Bree: What do you want me to say? My husband likes to wear metal clamps around his nipples. Hooray.

Rex: I want you to say you'll try it. Just, just once.

Bree: Try what? Hurting you? You actually want me to hurt you?

Rex: So I can feel pleasure, yes.

Bree: Fine.

(Bree slaps him.)

Bree: So? Was it good for you, too? ("Love Is in the Air," 1–14)

The clip freezes, and then fades back to the still photo of Bree. The panel is uncharacteristically quiet.

"Any comments?" the Host asks. "Fred, you're not usually at a loss for words."

"Can you rewind to that part where she drops the fur coat? I think we need to see that again," Fred says.

"That's my kind of girl," Billy says, winking again. "Homina, homina, homina."

"If I had a body like that, I'd walk around in my underwear all day long," Patricia says.

"If you had a body like that, people might actually stop mistaking you for a man," Fred retorts, drawing mild laughter from the audience. Patricia crosses her arms and looks annoyed.

"Charles, any thoughts?" the Host asks quickly, before Patricia can retaliate.

"Obviously, the point you're trying to make is that in the second set of clips, Bree appears to be a much different woman than in the first set of clips. She's earthier, lustier," Charles says. "But I'm not buying it. I don't think that the woman in the second set of clips is fundamentally different from the homemaker shown in the first set of clips. The point being made is that sometimes she's domestic, and sometimes she's sexual. Well, what about it? Aren't most people different in the bedroom than they are in other areas of their life?"

"That hasn't been my experience," Fred argues. "Most of the women I've dated have had the same personality in and out of the bedroom. Shy, outgoing, adventurous... they don't change suddenly when they get between the sheets."

Patricia rolls her eyes.

"Billy?" the Host asks.

"This reminds me of a joke I once heard. A priest, a rabbi and a duck all go into a bar," Billy begins, flashing his famous dimples.

"Oh dear, I don't think we'll have time for that," the Host says. "Right now, we need to take a break to hear from our sponsors."

The shows theme music starts playing.

"And, cut the tape," a producer yells from the front.

"What the hell was that?" Billy asks. Now that the camera isn't rolling, the big smile has disappeared, replaced by a sullen frown. "Why'd you cut off my joke?"

"Because if we had to hear another one of your priest and rabbi jokes, we'd lose our collective minds," Charles replies.

"Those jokes are my fucking trademark," Billy snarls.

The audience murmurs with alarm at his salty language. Billy's well known as a squeaky-clean, family-friendly comedian who often shows up on the late night talk shows.

"Well, I for one didn't appreciate Fred's comments about my appearance. Why is he allowed to get away with it? Just the other day, the producer reprimanded me for making an innocuous joke about Fred, but he's allowed to get away with trash-talking me?"

"Innocuous joke? You called me a 'girly-man' on the air," Fred says.

"Big deal. They edited it out," Patricia replies.

"Is this tap water?" Charles asks, staring at the glass of water one of the production assistants has handed him. "I wanted Evian." He takes a sip and shudders.

The Host ignores them all. He's too busy examining his reflection in the hand mirror an assistant is holding up for him, while one of the stylists dabs at his face with a cosmetic sponge.

"And we're back to tape in five, four..." the producer shouts out. The assistants and stylist run off the stage. "...three, two, on air!"

The music cues up again, and the Host turns his cheesy grin toward the camera.

"Welcome back to *Which One Is It?!*" he says enthusiastically. "The game that's all about separating the real contestant from the imposters! Usually, our panel of experts questions three individuals who are all claiming to be the contestant, and tries to figure out which one is the real contestant. But on today's show we're trying something a little different. We're showing video clips of one Bree Van De Kamp," the Host says, waving at the television sets, all displaying the picture of the frozen Bree, "in different situations, and asking them to figure out who the real Bree is. So far, we've seen a domestic Bree..."

"The Stepford Wife," Patricia interjects.

"...and we've seen Bree as a coquette," the Host continues.

"Va-va-voom," Fred says.

"Now in our final set of clips, we're going to see yet another side of Bree Van De Kamp. Are you ready, panel?" the Host asks.

The panel nods.

"Then let's roll the final set of clips," the Host chirps. He hits the play button on his remote control one last time.

The video on the third and final television begins to play. The frozen shot of Bree disappears, and in its place is a video clip of Bree sitting down next to her son, Andrew, in a seedy strip club. Andrew is visibly annoyed at his mother's presence.

ANDREW: What are you doing?

BREE: I'm staying for the show. I'm dying to see what all the fuss is about. Excuse me, waitress, I'll have a glass of your house chardonnay. I'm curious, Andrew, as you fantasize about this woman, do you ever stop and think how she came to be on this runway? That's someone's little girl. And that someone probably had a lot of dreams for her...dreams that did not include a thong and a pole.

ANDREW: It's not going to work, okay? I'm not budging.

BREE: God only knows what she's had to deal with in her life....Poverty? Drugs? Domestic violence? Maybe even molestation.

ANDREW: Mom!

BREE: And now she treats herself the way that other men treat her. Like an object, a piece of meat.

PATRON: That's it, kid. Get her out of here. She's killing it for the rest of us. ("Who's That Woman?" 1–4)

In the next clip, Bree is standing in Rex's hospital room. He's lying in bed, looking sickly, and Bree sits down on the edge of his bed and leans close to her husband.

BREE: I know you still love me. Maisy told me.

REX: She did?

BREE: As of this moment, Rex, I am no longer your wife. I am going to go out, and find the most vindictive lawyer I can find, and together, we are going to eviscerate you. I'm going to take away your money, your family, and your dignity. Do you hear me?

REX: Bree....

BREE: And I am so thrilled to know that you still love me. Because I want what's about to happen to you to hurt as much as is humanly possible. I'm so glad you didn't die before I got a chance to tell you that.

(BREE stands up, and stalks out of the room, her face cold.) ("Come Back to Me," 1–10)

In the final clip, Gabby is sitting on her front porch. Bree strolls down the front walk, and steps up onto the porch.

GABBY: Bree, hi.
BREE: Hi.
GABBY: What's up?
BREE: Well, um, I've been doing some thinking. Rex and I have been members of the Fairview Country Club for years, and, well, lately, it seems to have lost some of its exclusivity, and so I've decided not to renew our membership. I'd rather see the money go to someone I care about.

(BREE hands GABBY an envelope. GABBY opens it and takes out a check.)

GABBY: Oh, Bree, I can't take that.
BREE: Gabby, this is the way I see it—good friends offer to help in a crisis. Great friends don't take no for an answer. ("The Ladies Who Lunch," 1–16)

The clip ends and, yet again, the television freezes back to the original picture of Bree.

"She's a spitfire," Billy says.

"I like this side of her more," Patricia says with grudging approval. "She's got balls."

"Lovely," Charles says, shooting Patricia a dirty look.

"What? All I'm saying is that she's showing a little backbone now," Patricia retorts.

"What did I say? They're all the same, whether in or out of bed," Fred says.

Patricia gapes at him, outrage contorting her features, but the Host steps in before she can speak.

"Billy, do you think that the Bree in the last set of clips is fundamentally different from the Bree in the first two sets of clips?" the Host asks.

"The way I see it is this: You've got your fifties-era housewife, your sexpot and your spitfire. So the question is, can one person be all of those things at once?" Billy asks.

"That's exactly it," Charles says, looking pleased for the first time since the show has begun. "The whole question of who's the real Bree suggests that there are three different choices and that only one of those choices can be the true essence of the woman. I disagree with the hypothesis."

"So, the woman's a doormat one minute, and telling off her husband the next?" Patricia asks, looking doubtful. "I think the chick has multiple personalities. Hey, is that the answer?"

"No," the Host says.

"I don't think she was a doormat in the first clips," Charles says. "She was simply behaving cordially, practicing the lost art of good manners."

"Believe it or not, I think I might actually agree with Patricia," Fred says. Everyone, especially Patricia, looks shocked. "The woman in the first set of clips was guarded. Her husband was right; it was like she was using domestic issues to distance herself. And then all of a sudden she's sitting in a restaurant talking about scrotums?"

"But these clips weren't put in context. We don't know what happened between the time when the family was sitting around eating soup and the point where Bree's standing in her husband's hospital room telling him she wants him to drop dead," Billy says.

"I can help there. Bree found out that her husband was having an affair with the neighborhood prostitute. He was paying her to, erm, dominate him," the Host says.

Patricia whistles. "Well, there you have it. I'd slap him across the face, too."

"That would certainly explain the change in her behavior," Billy agrees.

"Maybe we should take a look at the clip of her in her underwear again," Fred says.

"Give it up, Fred," Patricia says.

"I still don't think it is a change. Where is it written that a woman can't be strong, sexy and yet still enjoy cooking?" Charles says.

"I don't think she does enjoy it," Patricia says. "She seemed so plastic and tense in the first set of clips, where she was giving out muffins and fixating on the doctor's button. She was smiling, but it looked forced, like she was really just gritting her teeth."

"That's just it. She seemed at her most comfortable at the very end, when she was giving her friend the check," Billy agrees.

"Perhaps," Charles says, although he still doesn't look convinced. "I still say that each of the three sets of clips we saw didn't show a fundamentally different woman."

"Panel, have you made your decision? Which set of clips do you think shows the real Bree? One, two or three?"

"Number three," Patricia says. "I hope. That's the Bree I liked best."

"Three," Billy agrees.

"Two," Fred says. "I vote for the lingerie."

"All three," Charles says stubbornly.

"You have to pick one," Patricia reminds him.

"No, I don't," he says,

"Yes, you do," she says. "It's in our contract."

"Fine," Charles says, folding his arms and looking petulant. "Number one."

"So it's that time," the Host says chirpily. A drum roll sounds, and spotlights begin swirling around the three televisions. "Will the real Bree please stand up?"

Nothing happens.

"Ummm," the Host says. "Let's try this again. Will the real Bree Van De Kamp please stand up?"

Again, nothing.

"I think I see the flaw in this new format," Charles says dryly.

But then, the televisions start to flicker. The still photo of Bree fades away from each screen, and is replaced by a silent montage of the scenes that were played earlier for the panel. Television one freezes on a shot of Bree in her proper funeral attire, holding out a basket of baked goods, a brittle smile on her face. Television two, to Fred's obvious delight, stills at the scene of Bree in her red lacey bra and panties, just seconds after she's shed her fur coat. Television three stops at the shot of Bree leaning over Rex's hospital bed, her face cold with rage.

The audience is silent, breathless even, as they wait. Then the three still images of Bree flash. On and off. On and off. For just a moment, the picture on television number two is still, while the other two go blank. The audience gasps. Is the real Bree the saucy minx? But no, television two fades away, and then the only picture on is number three, showing Bree in her scorned woman fury.

"I knew it!" Patricia crows.

But as soon as the words have left her lipstick-ringed mouth, television number three fades away. A recorded drum roll beings to play . . . the houselights dim, and three spotlights begin to wildly circle the televisions . . . the theme music swells over the sound of the drums . . . .

"They're really drawing this out," Billy comments.

Suddenly all three televisions go blank. The drum roll ends abruptly with the ringing of a cymbal. The spotlights still, casting a pool of light on each television set. And then, one by one, the televisions light up. They're again all showing the same still photo of Bree...only this time it's the picture of her at Mary Alice Young's funeral, offering the basket of muffins to Paul Young.

"And the real Bree Van De Kamp is number one!" the Host exclaims.

The audience applauds and murmurs among itself.

"I was right!" Charles exclaims.

Patricia looks vexed. "Oh, come on! That Bree was so plastic. The third one seemed much more real," she says.

"Why don't we get to know the real Bree Van De Kamp a little better?" the Host suggests. He presses a button on his remote control, and all three televisions begin to play the same montage of scenes.

Here's Bree prodding the family reverend to talk her son, Andrew, out of being gay. Here's Bree, back in the red lingerie, but this time the scene continues on, showing how she interrupted her lovemaking with Rex to clean up the cheese oozing out of his discarded burrito. Here's Bree smoothing the bed covers and plumping the pillows while Rex, suffering from a heart attack, sits and waits for her to drive him to the hospital. Here's Bree at her husband's funeral, so incensed at the tie her mother-in-law has dressed Rex in, she marches into the congregation and orders Tom Scavo to give her his tie, so that Rex's corpse can be properly outfitted when he's buried. As Bree walks out of the church after Rex's funeral, a victorious smile on her face, the picture again freezes.

"So that's it?" Patricia asks. "The real one is Charles' Stepford Wife?"

"Maybe," Fred says, in an uncharacteristic moment of insight, "that's just it. She can be a good friend or a sexy woman, but the anal-retentive side of her overshadows the other aspects of her personality."

The other three panelists stare at him for a long moment, all startled that Fred has so quickly put his finger on it. The Host is pleased; he nods approvingly at Fred.

"Like the scene with the burrito," Fred continues. "She was obviously intending to seduce Rex, but she couldn't let go of her control-freak tendencies. She was so obsessed with cleaning up the cheese it overrode her desire to get it on with her husband."

"I see what you're saying," Patricia says slowly. "It's not that she can't be a good friend or a sexually aware woman, just that those aren't her strongest traits."

"Very good," the Host says. "Charles, you were the only panelist to guess correctly. Any thoughts?"

Charles bridges his fingers together and looks thoughtful. "Actually, I think that I was wrong," he said.

"Charles admitting he's wrong…now that's a first," Billy says. "I'm going to need a tape of this show as proof that he actually said those words aloud."

Charles glares at Billy before continuing. "I didn't choose the first Bree because I thought her perfectionist tendencies control the other areas of her life. I chose her because I thought the first Bree seemed the most pleased with herself. When she was talking about sex or trying to seduce her husband or confronting her son at the strip club, she seemed a bit uncomfortable. Out of her element. But when Bree was engaged in domestic pursuits, she was in her glory. Her face lit up and her eyes sparkled."

"That's also when she looked the most like a Stepford Wife," Patricia says.

"I disagree," Charles says, shaking his head. "Stepford wives are glassy-eyed and vacant. Bree's just the opposite—she comes alive when she's taking care of her home and family. To build upon what Fred was saying about her being a—how did you put, Fred? You said she was 'a control freak'?"

Fred nods. "The chick *is* tightly wound. Remember how she was fixating on the doctor's button?"

"Indeed. Well, I think Bree probably does feel at her most comfortable when she's in control of her environment. She's a perfectionist," Charles says.

"So if Charles picked the right Bree for the wrong reason does it count?" Fred asks.

"Yes. It counts," the Host says. "And, anyway, I don't think that Charles did pick her for the wrong reason. His insights into Bree's character are quite interesting."

"Damn," Fred mutters.

"Well, I still think that it's the least attractive side of her personality. What sort of a modern woman is defined only by her role as a wife and mother?" Patricia asks. She scowls. "It's anti-feminist."

"I think there are a lot of women who define themselves by those roles," Billy says, suddenly more serious than usual. "Granted, most aren't as extreme as Bree, with her basil puree soup and baskets of muffins."

"And who's to say that it's anti-feminist, if being a homemaker is what makes her happy, and what works for her family?" Charles argues.

"But it wasn't working for her family," Patricia points out. "They were all miserable."

"Yeah, but they might have been just as hacked off if she'd been obsessing about her career, or about what shoes she was going to buy, instead of the button," Fred says.

Patricia considers this. "Maybe," she says, although she still sounds unconvinced.

Just then, a tired-sounding horn blows. *Poo-bah.*

"Well, folks, you know what that means. We're out of time for today," the Host says, grinning widely. "Thank you for watching *Which One Is It?*! Please join us again next time. And for now, toodle-oo!"

The Host throws an arm out in his signature wave, sweeping his arm in front of him as though drawing an upside down U. The audience applauds politely, and the stage lights go dark as the houselights rise.

"Is that it? Is it over?" the audience members ask one another. And when nothing else happens, they start to get up and shuffle toward the aisles. But over the din of footsteps on metal risers and coughs and the raised voices of the audience as they debate the outcome of the show, the panel's bickering voices can be heard.

"All I said was that I wouldn't mind having a photo of Bree in her underwear," Fred says. "I don't know why you have to make a federal case out of it."

"You're such a pig," Patricia snorts.

"Says you. No one else thinks so," Fred snaps back.

"Actually, I also think you're a pig," Charles says stiffly.

"Me three," Billy says.

"I am so out of here," the Host says. "I need a drink."

"Wait up, I'll join you," Patricia says. She smiles suggestively at the Host, and tucks her arm under his.

The Host looks a bit alarmed at the prospect. He fingers the knot in his tie.

"Erm," he says. "Well...I suppose. Maybe just a quick drink."

Billy claps the Host on the back, as the group slowly exits the stage. "Don't worry. We'll all come. Speaking of which, have you heard the joke about the priest, the rabbi and the game show host who go into the bar?"

Whitney Gaskell briefly—and reluctantly—practiced law, before publishing her first book, *Pushing 30.* She is also the author of *True Love (and Other Lies)*, *She, Myself & I* and the forthcoming *Testing Kate.* Whitney lives on the Treasure Coast of Florida with her husband and son. She is currently at work on her fifth book.

Whitney wishes she could be more like Bree—or, at least, she'd like to have an immaculate house and serve a gourmet meal every night—but sadly doesn't have the time or energy to do much more than run the vacuum once a week and order take-out.

You can find more about her books at www.whitneygaskell.com.

Michelle Cunnah

Desperately Seeking Susan

Susan Mayer's not the brightest crayon in the box, but she's awfully hard not to love. From her inexplicably endearing clumsiness to her helpless inability to make things work with Mike the Plumber, Susan's struggles elicit our sympathies in ways the other Housewives' can't quite match. Michelle Cunnah takes it a step further. When push comes to shove, Susan's the only Housewife Michelle would want in her corner—lousy relationship history, questionable parenting skills, botched good intentions and all.

W HEN I WAS ASKED to contribute to this anthology I had a tough time deciding which Desperate Housewife to write about, because for many reasons, at various times in their complicated lives (or, indeed, complicated deaths), I have alternately loved, hated, despised, gotten frustrated with and cheered on each of them.

But there's only one Desperate Housewife I would choose as a best friend. I asked myself what traits I hold dear in a best friend, and there are many, but the basic ones are these: that they are loyal, that they offer good advice and be there for me in my time of need, and that they would take great care of my kids if for some reason I could not.

I set about applying these conditions to the Desperate Housewives, examining their actions and reactions, how they conduct their lives, how they interacted with each other in season one, and I came to a conclusion that rather shocked me, and will probably shock you, too, and this is it:

If I had to pick the one Housewife I most admired, the one I would want guarding my back if I were in trouble, the one I would trust with my kids, the one I would turn to if I was in trouble, it would be Susan Mayer.

"But she's a ditz!" I hear you all cry. "Come on, Michelle, she gets advice about her sex life from her teenage daughter, for goodness sake. How can that be admirable?"

Yes, yes, yes. I know that Susan is a wacky, disorganized ditz, and her daughter Julie often appears to be the grownup in the mother-daughter relationship. I never said that Susan was the perfect mother. But she certainly isn't a bad one, either; look how well Julie has turned out so far.

"But how can you respect someone who sneaks into Edie's house thinking that Edie is having a wild night of passion with Mike, accidentally sets fire to Edie's house and then runs out without even warning Edie? Are you mad?"

Yes, I know that Susan often acts first and thinks later. I never said that she was a perfect adult with perfect reasoning skills, either. But just because Susan doesn't always control her impulses doesn't make her less admirable and trustworthy as a friend—many times she acts on impulse for the good of others, too, or at least what she thinks is for the good of others.

Before you all start throwing rotten tomatoes at me, come with me as I go in search of the real Susan Mayer—the woman behind the klutziness and the admittedly iffy snooping decisions.

Question: *If I were in need of relationship advice, which Housewife would I turn to?*

Mary Alice? At first glance she *seems* to be the perfect wife in a perfect family unit, but let's face it, she bowed out of her relationship with Paul by committing suicide. You don't bow out of a relationship more dramatically and finally than that.

If things had been that great between them, wouldn't she have spoken with Paul about being blackmailed? After all, Paul knew all about her past history—Zach's abduction, the murder—because Paul was an intrinsic part of it. So *why* didn't she just discuss the situation with him? Why did she effectively run away from him?

Gabrielle? Much as I love her, why would I consult a woman who married for money, doesn't really seem to love her husband and has affairs with underage boys? Can we say dysfunctional, here?

I mean, Gabrielle nearly let *Susan* take the rap for her affair with John. Nearly, but in the end she redeemed herself by confessing the truth. Even so, what advice could she give when her own relationships are such a tangled mess?

Lynette? On the surface she and her husband Tom seem to really love each other, so maybe she would be the perfect relationship guru. But if you look a little deeper, she did seem to spend a lot of her time in the first season worrying about whether or not (a) Tom was going to have an affair (look how quickly Lynette got rid of the nanny after Tom accidentally saw her nude), (b) Tom would get promoted to a job that meant he would have to travel a lot and therefore (in Lynette's mind) he would have an affair or (c) Tom would have an affair with his old flame.

Lynette manipulated the situation to such an extent that Tom lost a promotion and discovered that Lynette had sabotaged his career, causing a rift between them. It almost seemed as if she were trying to throw him into the Other Woman's arms. It was almost as if she *wanted* Tom to have an affair so that all of her fears would be true, and she would be proved *right*. She always has to be right, no matter what the cost to her relationship.

Bree? Ah, Bree, the loveable control freak, the neat freak, whose husband Rex left her and had sado-masochistic sex with another woman because Bree was too obsessed with order and neatness to consider varying their sex life, or any other area of their seemingly perfect existence, even a little.

Even when Bree tried to repair her relationship with Rex by turning up at his hotel room wearing a fur coat and little else in a quest to seduce him, she couldn't lose control for long enough to ignore the burrito that was about to fall on the hotel carpet. She completely ruined the moment, halting the seduction to catch the dripping cheese before it hit the floor.

But Susan? Well, as far as we know, Susan didn't cheat on her husband Karl—he was the one who left her, and for his secretary. Point to Susan.

As for her relationship with Mike? Although she may at times appear juvenile, all she really wants from Mike is his love. And that he not lie to her. The truth is very important to Susan.

How can you not love her when she douses herself in gravy in a bid to win the love of Mike's dog, and therefore the love of Mike? Of course, it backfired when Bongo accidentally swallowed one of her earrings along with the gravy. But this did show how Susan finds the courage to go after what she wants, even if it often leads to disaster.

And yes, when Susan had the keys to Mike's house so that she could let in the builder in Mike's absence, she went snooping and found a gun and a lot of money. But answer me this: If you were in a new relationship and had the keys to your loved one's house, wouldn't you go snooping just a bit? Just a very little bit? I'd love to be able to take the moral high ground and say, "Of course not," but a sneaky part of me would be tempted.

Susan's efforts to put her failed marriage behind her and move on were admirable. She apologized to Karl's girlfriend, Brandy, for all her bitchiness in her quest to achieve closure and, surprisingly, Brandy apologized right back for causing Susan pain.

Susan tried to be gracious to Karl when his relationship with Brandy broke up. She invited him to Julie's birthday party, and even when he brought Edie as a date Susan remained gracious. It was only when she discovered that Edie slept with Karl before the breakup of her marriage that Susan sought revenge by making a public scene. Although that scene made me cringe, it also made me want to applaud Susan for having the guts to do it.

When Karl apologized to Susan, and told her he wanted her back, that it was a mistake that they ever split up, we all worried that Susan would fall for his ruse (and fall back into his arms). I mean, she's supposed to be the weak Housewife, right? But Susan is much stronger than that—she knew that she truly *had* moved on, that she loved *Mike*, and she showed Karl the door.

And see how Susan fought for her relationship with Mike? When she thought that he was a drug dealer and murderer, she ended things with him because of what was seemingly irrefutable police evidence, but she couldn't just leave things as they were. Instead, she hired a private investigator, which led her ultimately to the truth about Mike: that he was not a murderer.

And when the Housewives staged an intervention (instigated by a jealous Edie) because they felt that Susan was rushing things—that she and Mike should not move in together so quickly—Susan defended Mike to the hilt. She would not be swayed from her belief in him.

Susan *wants* to believe. She *wants* to trust. She told the Housewives that she would expect the *best* from Mike. And I admire her for that.

Question: *If something happened to me, which Housewife would I trust with my children?*

Mary Alice? Mary Alice deserted her own child by killing herself. It doesn't matter what kind of great mother she was until that point; she chose to kill herself rather than remain with her child.

Although you have to wonder: Was she that great a mother in the first place? Zach, her son, is now a disturbed, violent teenager. Of course, much of Zach's behavior can be attributed to the loss of his biological mother, and the subsequent mystery surrounding her death, but can all of it? After all, he did witness his adopted mother, Mary Alice, killing his biological mother. He knew that something bad had happened, but mistakenly believed that *he* was the perpetrator. What kind of legacy is that to leave to your child?

Something which bothers me greatly is Mary Alice's choice of the toy box to conceal the chopped-up body of Zach's biological mother. How icky is it that Mary Alice even *thought* to do that?

Gabrielle? Self-confessedly she doesn't even like or want children, because she is totally selfish and self-centered (although she can show unselfish qualities when the occasion demands it). It is admirable that she knows this about herself, but she, too, would not be my first choice as a replacement mother. How could I trust her with *my* teenage son?

Lynette? Although she tries hard to be a good mother, the truth is that her brood of four are always out of control. She bribes, cajoles and often threatens them—threats that she never delivers on.

When Bree administered a spanking to one of Lynette's kids while looking after them, something that Lynette had often threatened to do, Lynette was furious. And how did she turn this around to her own advantage? When threatening her kids afterward Lynette told them that if they did not behave, *Bree* would spank them, *Bree* would punish them. Not her.

And what kind of mother pulls over her car and abandons her kids on the side of the road, even for a few minutes? Even to frighten them and teach them a lesson? We might all be tempted on occasion, but would we really deliberately place our children in danger like that? I think not. And in any case, it didn't work; Lynette's children continue to run riot.

Bree? When her teenage son (driving under the influence of alcohol) ran down Mrs. Solis, Bree took charge of the family and the crime was covered up. You can't help sympathizing with a mother who, after all, is just trying to protect her children. But Andrew, her son, didn't seem in the least bit remorseful, and Bree seemed more concerned with appearances than with understanding and helping her son.

And when Andrew confessed that he was gay, instead of supporting him, Bree was worried about what everyone would think. It is as if her family must be perfect at all costs, even if she has to sacrifice her son's true identity—his true feelings—and at the cost of his respect and love for her.

When Bree found some condoms and discovered that they belonged to her teenage daughter, instead of talking to Danielle rationally about safe sex, Bree flipped out. Again.

Would I trust Bree not to screw up my kids? We all make mistakes on occasion, no matter how much we try to be the perfect parent, but as much as I love Bree, the answer is a resounding no. Her first concern at any sign of trouble would not be about my kids' well-being, but their, and her, reputation. She would gloss over anything they did wrong in order to present the appearance of the perfect family to the rest of the world.

Susan? As many people said to me when I first approached this essay, Susan often reverses roles with her daughter; of the two of them, Julie often seems to be the adult. There was, for instance, the advice that Julie gave to her mom about sex. And when Susan had her first date with Mike, Julie checked that Susan had protection. But at least they *discuss* sex, and they care about each other, and look out for each other.

And yes, when Susan confessed to Julie that Mrs. Huber was blackmailing her, Julie's reaction was, "Why do I even let you out of the house?" But we can all sympathize with that, since we as viewers often feel the same way about Susan.

How did the Susan/Julie team resolve the blackmail issue? Julie snuck into Mrs. Huber's house to retrieve the burned measuring cup—the "evidence" that Susan was in Edie's house the night it burned down. Weren't mother and daughter, again, simply taking care of each other? The fact is that Julie is smaller and can fit through the dog flap, and if she was caught what was Mrs. Huber going to do? If Mrs. Huber called the police, the blackmail would end and Mrs. Huber would have lost out, so Julie wasn't in any real danger.

There's more great evidence that Susan and Julie are a real team, and loyal to each other. When they were having dinner at Mike's and Edie was trying to establish Susan as a recently separated woman not yet over her ex-husband, as part of her bid to win Mike for herself, Susan seemed incapable of turning the conversation around and defending herself. And so Julie stepped into the breach to defend her mother instead.

When Julie really needs Susan to be responsible, she is. It was Susan who forbade Zach and Julie to see each other, because she was concerned about Zach's state of mind (and that he may have accidentally killed his baby sister). And when Zach came to see Susan and became violent, Susan was strong and ordered him out of her house. Julie didn't like it, but Susan (although admitting that she behaves like a teenager on occasion) stuck to her guns. She protected her daughter.

Later, when Julie was looking for a way to end things with Zach without hurting him even more, Susan took the blame with Zach for the breakup.

When Susan's ditzy mother Sophie moved in, Susan immediately switched into maternal mode, taking responsibility for her, making sure she was safe and trying to save her from her own irrationality, all while shielding Julie from Sophie's indiscretions. Susan herself has admitted that, "I think it's nature's little joke—that children ultimately end up parenting their parents." But with this family, you can see it working both ways. And working well.

Whether we approve or disapprove of Susan's specific mothering choices, at the end of the day her daughter is the happiest, most well-adjusted child on Wisteria Lane. So would I trust Susan with my kids? You bet.

Question: *If I was desperately in need of a loyal friend, which House-wife would I completely trust to be there for me?*

Although all of the Desperate Housewives missed Mary Alice and wanted to find out what really happened to her, none of them wanted to do so as much as Susan. At least, none of them pursued it with as much passion as Susan.

At Mary Alice's wake, Susan immediately voiced her suspicions that there was more to Mary Alice's death than they knew. And when the Desperate Housewives discovered the blackmail note, it was Susan who asked, "Mary Alice, what did you do?" Susan may not always think as carefully as she should before attempting to dig up secrets, but in doing so, regardless of the risk, she shows an amazing loyalty to her friends.

It was Susan who insisted that the Housewives go ahead with Mary Alice's dinner party, and in the middle of a very uncomfortable scene between Bree and Rex, it was Susan who (loyally) attempted to defuse the situation by relating the tale of getting herself locked outside naked. She made a fool of herself to help her friend, and I have to love her for that.

When Gabrielle discovered that she was pregnant, Susan was the first on the scene to comfort her. When Lynette became overwhelmed with motherhood and her Ritalin addiction, Susan was the first to find her and offer her support. And when Rex had a heart attack, Susan was the first one to arrive at the hospital to comfort Bree.

Susan's loyalty gives her keen instincts when it comes to the people she cares about—and she's not afraid to follow those instincts, no matter how dangerous or ill-advised it might seem. Susan suspected that Paul was lying to her about Zach's whereabouts, and wanted to see Zach for herself in order to establish that no harm had come to him. So she borrowed a neighbor's car, put on a disguise and followed Paul. Ultimately, because of her irrational suspicion and rash actions, she discovered where Zach was and was able to send her daughter into the hospital to establish that Zach was basically okay.

After Paul told Susan that Zach accidentally killed Dana, Susan was again suspicious. When she told this to Edie, Edie suggested that they snoop inside Paul's house using Edie's spare key and Susan agreed, without a thought of her own safety, because she is tenaciously loyal. She wanted to know the truth about Mary Alice, and felt she owed it to Mary Alice to do so, even if it meant taking personal risks.

When Paul discovered what Susan had done and spun her another explanation that included an implied physical threat, Susan still didn't abandon Mary Alice or her quest to discover the truth about her friend's death. What did she do? Once more, she trusted her instincts. She hired a private investigator (albeit the wrong one) to establish the truth. How many people would do that just for friendship's sake?

When Susan found Mrs. Huber's journal in Mike's van, she couldn't resist sneaking off and reading it herself. But when she discovered the truth about the deaths of Mary Alice and Mrs. Huber, she wanted to do the morally right thing, even if it meant risking her relationship with Mike. She ultimately got Mike to agree to take the journal to the police.

Susan is sometimes ditzy, often attracts drama and doesn't always think things through before she leaps into a situation, but she is always true and loyal, and always just *there* for her friends, even if they're dead. She might not be the best mother, but she always comes through when her daughter needs her. She might make mistakes in her relationships, but she always sets out to believe the best, and her instincts are often proved right.

In short, Susan is someone I would be proud to call a friend and, in desperately seeking Susan, I hope that I've found at least a little part of her.

Michelle Cunnah loves and empathizes with Susan more than the other Housewives because she often feels like Susan's less wacky, not-quite-as-accident-prone older sister. But in a "Michelle's life has way less drama" kind of way. You can find out more about Michelle's antics at http://www.literarychicks.com.

Originally from England, Michelle spent six years living just outside Manhattan. She has lived in quite a lot of other places, too. Currently, she can be found weebling ineptly along the cycle lanes in Rotterdam, the Netherlands.

The award-winning author of *32AA*, *Call Waiting* and *Confessions of a Serial Dater*, she can also be found on the Web at http://www.michelle-cunnah.com.

Sharon Bowers

"I Bet You Were a Cheerleader"
Outside Looking In on Wisteria Lane

Television shows, unlike books and movies, are subject to the realities of their actors' lives; often, actors are ready to leave a show before it makes sense for their character to do so, leaving the writers scrambling to smooth over the disruption in the plot. But the narrative flexibility that serial television's long runs require can also be a boon, allowing shows to incorporate characters and plotlines they never anticipated as actors become available and stories develop in unexpected ways. Edie Britt was supposed to be a one-shot, a pilot episode nemesis to introduce conflict to the plot and highlight Susan's wholesome Midwestern cheerleader appeal. But she did it so well that Marc Cherry and his team decided to keep Nicollette Sheridan on, and now it's difficult to imagine Desperate Housewives *without her. Without Edie, Sharon Bowers asserts, the show would lose more than a snarky outsider perspective on the House-wives' lives. Without Edie, the show would lose* viewers.

"What the hell kinda street do we live on?"

Desperate Housewives debuted in September of 2004 to almost immediate widespread acclaim from critics who enjoyed the show's sly use of satire to comment on the nature of suburban life, while audiences were intrigued at the genre-bending blend of comedy, mystery and soap opera. By far, the bulk of the press and public's attention was focused on the four "Desperate Housewives" of the title, but there was one more major female character—Edie Britt—who was neither desperate nor interested in being a housewife.

In his commentary for the pilot episode of the series, creator and writer Marc Cherry said, "This part was just a guest spot in the original pilot and Nicollette popped for us in such a way that we decided, 'Nope, we've got to have her back for the entire series.'" Her entrance into the text without a defined narrative arc was Edie's first destabilizing act. She was never meant to exist within the narrative and thus, from the beginning, she has stood outside it. This had important implications for both the text and the viewers throughout the first season of *Desperate Housewives*.

"Susan had met the enemy—and she was a slut."

The recently deceased Mary Alice Young's voice from beyond the grave provides a narrative guide throughout the series, and her descriptions established Edie in a powerful juxtaposition to the other "housewives" of Wisteria Lane. In "She Says, He Says: The Power of the Narrator in Modernist Film Politics," B. Ruby Rich argues that the voice-over narrator "holds a position of omniscience...privy to information unavailable to the film's characters and inaccessible within the film text. In this guise, the narrator quickly becomes the favored replacement for the viewer in search of identification." Indeed, through Mary Alice's descriptions and ethereal "authority," the audience had already been introduced to perfectionist Bree Van De Kamp, overwhelmed stay-at-home mom Lynette Scavo, former model turned trophy wife Gabrielle Solis and longing-for-true-love single mom Susan Mayer—four very good friends who were shocked and saddened by Mary Alice's unexpected suicide. Thus Mary Alice's description of Edie as a "slut" and an "enemy" of Susan located Edie firmly in the position of "outsider" on Wisteria Lane. Of her, Mary Alice said, "Edie Britt was the most predatory divorcee in a five-block radius. Her conquests were numerous, varied and legendary," while accompanying visuals depicted Edie seducing a handyman, a tennis coach and a minister in turn ("Pilot," 1–1). Indeed, from the little the audience had seen, new Wisteria Lane resident and house plumber extraordinaire Mike Delfino seemed to be just Edie's type. That Susan, an insider on the lane (not to mention first billed in the credits), also set her sights on Mike created an immediate tension within the text involving Susan and Edie.

This tension provided more than just the comic relief of the occasional bitchy insult-slinging to the text. Far more importantly, it emphasized the main narrative theme of "something rotten in the state of Suburbia." Just as Mary Alice wasn't what she seemed—a woman with a loving and picture-perfect family—Edie's presence as Susan's doppelganger reminded viewers that the housewives too may not be what they seemed, even to themselves. It also provided the first wedge allowing viewers who didn't read "with"—didn't identify with—Mary Alice and her merry band of housewives to find a place with and investment in the *Desperate Housewives* text. That place was Edie Britt.

"I really want to like you, Susan."

By positing Edie and Susan as polar opposites, *Desperate Housewives* tapped into one of the oldest narrative tropes there is: the struggle between "good" girls and "bad" ones. Though talking about film noir, Janey Place's statement, "[W]oman here as elsewhere is defined by her sexuality: the dark lady has access to it and the virgin does not" holds true for a range of texts. That the "dark lady" in question in *Desperate Housewives* is a blonde doesn't make any difference. Edie demonstrates her access to her sexuality by her willingness to expose her body, by her frank expression of sexual desire and by her confidence and self-possession. Susan, by contrast, denies access to her sexuality through her celibacy following her divorce, her embarrassment when her body is exposed and her awkwardness and clumsiness in general. Yet in her very ordinariness, Susan is celebrated and textually defined as being an insider on Wisteria Lane, whereas Edie is couched in monstrous terms. In "Ah, But Underneath" (1–2), when Mike asked Susan if Edie liked steaks, she answered, "Oh yes, she's definitely a carnivore."

The identification of Edie's (textually defined) excessive sexuality as "monstrous" further opened the text to other "outsider" viewers whose sexuality is societally defined as "monstrous." Though he has created a show ostensibly focused on a group of heterosexual women, Marc Cherry is not unaware of the presence of alternative readings of his text or the viewers who might identify with them. In addition to speaking at various gay and lesbian panels on television, Cherry has famously remarked of his show, "There's something about a woman mowing her lawn in an evening gown that's inherently gay." Because of the text's continual emphasis on her sexuality and her "performance" of femininity (as discussed later), Edie becomes a logical focal point for these and other kinds of "against the grain" readings and viewers. The act of "reading against the grain" has its origins in feminist theory and, at its heart, involves reading texts in any way not necessarily intended by the texts' authors. This form of "oppositional reading" is valuable not just because it offers marginalized readers/viewers a point of view within a text, but also because it opens up a text to a variety of interpretations and cultural connections. For *Desperate Housewives*, these sorts of readings become even more valuable because, at its heart, the narrative itself seeks to interrogate what lies beneath the perfectly manicured lawns and in the basements of these snug houses; the show, in effect, seeks its own alternate reading of the placid surface of Suburbia.

Much is made of Edie's vaunted number of lovers, and yet, ironically, she is the only character who did not have an on-screen love scene during the entire first season. Viewers "heard" Edie having sex in the pilot episode, and as a result of this one-night stand her house was burned down, albeit inadvertently, by good-girl Susan who jealously and mistakenly assumed that Mike was the unseen man in Edie's bed. Thus, while the text acknowledges and allows for the possibility of the alternativity of guilt-free, non-monogamous sexual freedom, it still keeps the idea very much contained. Edie's punishment for this alternativity was to remain homeless and on the fringes of Wisteria Lane—much like the viewers who identify with her—for the rest of the season. The text further emphasized its containment of transgression in the episode "The Ladies Who Lunch" (1–16). Perfect housewife turned prostitute Maisy Gibbons was arrested for providing "professional" sexual relief to some of Wisteria Lane's more frustrated husbands—including Bree's husband, Rex. Like Edie, in each of her appearances Maisy served as a doppelganger to one of the main housewives. In her first appearance, "Running to Stand Still" (1–6), her involved-school-mom perfection drove Lynette to pills in order to keep up with her. By her second appearance in "Come Back to Me" (1–10), however, Maisy's fortunes had changed. Her husband had lost his prominent position at the bank, and Maisy had turned to the world's oldest profession to make ends meet and, more importantly, keep up appearances. In this she differed from Edie—whose only interest in "appearances" is the one in her mirror—but the characters paralleled each other in that they were, as a result of their transgressions, both relegated to the "outside." They no longer conformed to the norm that Wisteria Lane represented, a status made explicit through their outlaw sexuality.

"Come Back to Me" paired Maisy not with sexually satisfied Lynette, but rather with Bree, whose housewifely perfection, we learned, did not extend into the bedroom. In "The Ladies Who Lunch," Maisy's transgressions caught up with her, and she was arrested. Panicked that Maisy's little black book would reveal Rex's infidelity, Bree visited Maisy in prison bearing her perfect muffins along with a bribe offer to remove Rex's name from her files. Echoing Edie calling out Susan's hypocrisy in "Every Day a Little Death" (1–12), Maisy did the very same thing to Bree. When Bree protested that they used to be friends, Maisy scornfully asked, "Where were you with your big basket of muffins when Harold lost his job and you knew we couldn't pay our bills?" She ended their encounter by acknowledging—as Edie did—her outsider status, calling herself "the town whore."

An argument can be made that Maisy's real transgression was choosing the terms, the price and, most importantly, the place of her sexual expression. For in violating the social and moral norms within Wisteria Lane, she was not only jailed but also, more importantly, in terms of the narrative, expelled from the community.

By contrast Susan's agency to her sexuality is tied up with traditional values of heterosexual marriage, and she is appropriately rewarded for them as she escapes punishment for the literal crime of arson. In "Pretty Little Picture" (1–3), the Housewives planned a dinner party. Answering Gabrielle's question "[There will be] three couples and Susan. Does that sound right?" Susan sighed and confessed, "That sounds very wrong." Her identification with and investment in traditional monogamy was most powerfully articulated in "Goodbye for Now" (1–22) when the wives attempted to talk Susan out of continuing her involvement with Mike because of his unexplained past. Susan refused their entreaties and, after talking about how hurt she'd been and for how long, declared, "When Mike asked me to move in with him, I was just happy...just ridiculously happy. I still am. I want to go with that feeling. I love him and...I *love* him. So I'm gonna expect the best from Mike, and I know that he's going to deliver that in return." The wives were moved by Susan's heartfelt words and similarly mirror Susan's moral investments, ultimately agreeing that Mike is "The One" for Susan, despite the fact that his status as a murderer is unresolved. Edie's response, on the other hand, was to roll her eyes and snark, "This is the worst intervention I've ever been to." Appropriately, Edie felt the need to "intervene" in the traditional path to heterosexual love, once again situating her "outside" the norm in her recognition that a path to true love strewn with accusations of murder might not be the best path to take.

"Every time I see those big doe eyes of hers,
I just want to go out and shoot a deer."

In her groundbreaking work on film "Visual Pleasure and Narrative Cinema," Laura Mulvey argues that one of the most powerful pleasures of film is a "pleasure in looking" (scopophilia), and, further, that historically this pleasure has chiefly been that of the male viewer, both on screen and off, looking at the female object. "The determining male gaze projects its fantasy onto the female figure, which is styled accordingly. In their traditional exhibitionist role women are simultaneously looked at and displayed, with their appearance coded for strong visual and erotic impact so that they can be said to connote *to-be-looked-at-ness*." In *Desperate Housewives*, that "to-be-looked-at-ness" would seem to be overturned, or at the very least subverted, because the text's main points of view consist of women: Susan, Bree, Lynette and Gabrielle—and most importantly, Mary Alice in her position "on high."

Much has been made in the press about the "men of *Desperate Housewives*" and their appeal as erotic spectacle. Indeed the show does play with this subversion of the traditional active "male" look in the amount of flesh that Gabrielle's "boytoy" John displays. However, the most important looks are reserved for and between the women themselves—frequently at the expense of their pleasure in looking at men.

In an important scene in the series' fourth episode, "Who's That Woman?" Susan lustfully stared at Mike's bare, muscular chest as he worked on his lawn. On the surface her gaze seemed to be a continuation of the series' reversal of the traditional active and passive gender roles. Her bliss at his masculine perfection was short-circuited, however, by the arrival of Edie across the street, not quite as scantily clad as Mike, in the process of washing her car. The camera cut shot-counter-shot-shot between the three characters, with Mike and Susan staring at Edie, who in turn pretended to be oblivious to both of them. Interestingly enough, once Edie was present on the scene, Susan's gaze fixed on Edie alone. She gave almost a play-by-play summary of Edie's actions, including a remark about Edie's "big guns," which only emphasized the intensity with which she was watching her "competition." Only when Susan's daughter Julie prompted her to go ask Mike out did she seem to even remember that Mike was there. The exchange of glances was made equal when Susan stormed out of her house to "return" Mike's stolen mail, and she and Edie stared at each other during her entire walk.

Susan and Edie's exchange of glances remains a visual theme throughout the series. In the episode "Anything You Can Do" (1–7), Edie watched

Susan on her way to her big date with Mike and remarked, "Wow, get a load of you. Don't you look pretty?" before adding, in typical Edie fashion, "I almost didn't recognize you." Her comment mirrored Mike's, "That is an amazing dress," and paralleled a similar disappointment as Mike cancelled their date because of the mysterious arrival of a woman from his past. By pairing Mike and Edie's comments, the difference between the male and female gaze in the *Desperate Housewives* text was made clear. Edie's gaze encompassed Susan entirely—she looked Susan over from head to toe as she spoke. Mike's gaze, however, focused on Susan's body, prominently displayed by her "great dress." Edie's comment is about Susan. Mike's comment is about Susan's adornment—adornment designed specifically to elicit the male gaze and sexually arouse.

The visual time and energy that the text spent on the two women looking at each other, rather than the mutual object of their affection, creates a disruption in the narrative. In these scenes the viewer's attention draws away from what they *should* be looking at—Susan's attraction to Mike—and focuses instead on Susan's attention (coded as antagonism) to Edie. In addition to creating a pleasurable viewing space for those not invested in the heterosexual narrative, the amount of time the women spend looking at each other—instead of at men, and instead of being looked at *by* men—subtly challenges the terms and meaning of pleasure in looking.

Because, in part, she stands outside the values of Wisteria Lane, Edie's gaze is also truthful, albeit sometimes painful. In "The Ladies Who Lunch," Edie listened impatiently to a depressed Susan mope about her breakup with Mike before rousting her out of the house because "Happy Hour started forty-five minutes ago." Sending Susan off to the showers with a slap on the derriere, she ordered her, "Don't forget to do something about that skanky hair. You're a little scary looking." Edie's command led the two ladies to a bar where, sitting side by side (a "two-shot," a standard cinematic signifier for a "couple"), they surveyed the trolling men—Edie with predatory glee at new blood, Susan with despair over losing Mike. Although Edie pointed out various, and more importantly, off-screen men, her attention was clearly focused on Susan.[1]

---

[1] The episode also notably marked Edie's first inclusion and involvement in attempting to solve the mystery of Mary Alice's suicide, further integrating her into the text and situating her to more firmly act as a transgressive mirror to Susan. The same episode featured a comic-hijink exercise in which Susan and Edie broke into Paul Young's house in an attempt to discover what he was hiding. There, they discovered a tape of Mary Alice at a birthday party being called "Angela," thus giving the Housewives one more important clue. Edie's prowess at "performing femininity" was also highlighted when she and Susan were almost caught by Paul. Edie came on sexually to Paul, kissing him provocatively until Susan had a chance to escape.

"She looks like fun!"

In "Notes on Camp," Susan Sontag defines "camp" as depending on the extravagant, the exaggerated and the theatrical. Similarly, Parker Tyler, in talking about "the Garbo Image," states, "Garbo 'got in drag' whenever she took some heavy glamour part.... It is all *impersonation*, whether the sex underneath is true or not." In *Desperate Housewives*, the repeated emphasis on people "looking" at Edie brings to the fore the concept of visual performance and is made more interesting because some of these viewers—Susan most notably—are women. Returning to Mulvey and the idea of the male spectator, Edie is very conscious of her "to-be-looked-at-ness." In her choice of clothing, of hairstyles, of words and of walk, Edie is continually linked with visual excess, but a calculated and, hence, knowing one. In "Goodbye For Now," Mary Alice commented, "Edie Britt's favorite moment of every day was her arrival at the construction site...because she knew what was about to happen. Her sudden appearance was always sure to garner a few appreciative glances, a few lascivious looks and some downright ogling." She derives a sense of satisfaction not just from the looks themselves, but because she controls them. When propositioned by a man she wasn't interested in, she dismissed him curtly, "Honey, you are so out of your league you aren't even playing the same sport." By recognizing Edie's performance of femininity—her enjoyment at being "ogled" and hence at putting on a show—the text inadvertently destabilizes the meaning of "femininity" and calls into question its position within heterosexuality in the text. Because Edie is defined as heterosexual, yet still "plays" at being a female for men and for Susan and the housewives also, the text keeps a (contained) place open for other constructions and interpretations of femininity.

A scene from "Anything You Can Do" further emphasized Edie's ability to control her "performance" in front of Susan. Worried about the arrival of a mysterious woman from Mike's past, Susan was content to wring her hands in despair, while Edie suggested a more proactive approach and coerced Susan into following Mike and the woman. Their plans went awry when Mike confronted Susan at the country and western bar where they all ended up. Although Edie was clearly in the background, Susan denied that Edie was there with her. The camera then followed Mike and Susan's gazes as they focused on Edie, hands on hips, smoothly riding in a manner that was both homage and parody of Debra Winger's bull ride in *Urban Cowboy*. Edie drew even more attention to herself, and to the fact that she and Susan had come together, by tossing her cowboy hat to Susan, who continued foolishly to deny that Mike was the reason she and Edie were at the bar. "I came to ride the bull," she insisted, stuffing Edie's cowboy hat on her head and beginning an awkward imitation of Edie's performance. She ripped the bottom half of her shirt open, tied it underneath her breasts and hurled her purse at Mike's stomach. She then slung her hat off and accidentally hit the operator of the bull, knocking him sideways into the controls. The mechanical bull abruptly jerked around and smacked her in the head, flattening her. The camera then cut to Susan sitting miserably between Mike and his lady friend, a bottle of beer pressed to her aching head.

"I bet you used to be a cheerleader."

What Susan's character seems to fail to grasp—even though the text very much does—is that Edie's ability to control her performance, and thus the gazes around her, is rooted in knowledge. More specifically: truth. The telling of lies and the revelation of truth are important themes in *Desperate Housewives*. In the Susan/Edie narrative, they are explored ironically through Edie's insistence on telling the truth and Susan's inclination to lie. For viewers who identify with one or more of the outsider values that Edie embodies, the recognition of truth and the ability to tell it about oneself is vital because that recognition is the apparatus that places them outside the norm. At the same time it destabilizes what the norm is because the alignment of Edie with truth and Susan with lie disrupts the position of all the Housewives as privileged.

In the aforementioned episode, Edie's reaction when she was busted, as recounted by Mike, was "Oops, game's up. I'm going to go ride the bull." Even though she was ostensibly "caught," she took control of the situation by admitting her transgression—following Mike—and moving on—riding the bull. On the other hand, Susan continued to lie to Mike and, in doing so, made a fool of herself.

The text clearly links Edie's knowing performance with her truth telling. In "The Ladies Who Lunch," she blithely retouched her lipstick while telling Paul that he has to disclose that Mary Alice killed herself in the house to any potential buyers. Ironically, Edie's penchant for telling the truth even when it means admitting something less than flattering about herself saved her life in the same episode. After finding the same kind of stationery in Edie's portfolio that was used to send a blackmail note to his wife, Paul dispatched a hired killer to "take care" of Edie. When the killer, who Edie thought was a real estate developer, inquired about the stationery, she easily admitted that she stole it from her friend

Mrs. Huber. The killer backed off, and Edie was spared. Contrast this with Susan's mistaken assumption that Mike was in Edie's bed, which led to the burning down of Edie's house and the series of lies that Susan had to tell, as well as Susan being blackmailed by Mrs. Huber, in an attempt to evade the truth. Susan's lies only led to more and compounded trouble, ultimately resulting in her being at Edie's mercy once her "guilt" finally overwhelmed her, some eleven episodes later. Edie, by not "fibbing" about the stationery, not only avoided complications, but also escaped unscathed from the hands of a killer for hire.

Of course, in a text like *Desperate Housewives*, the truth always comes out, and in the Susan/Edie narrative, the revelation of the truth and the knowledge it brings returned the arc to the insider/outsider theme with which it began. Detoured by a flat tire on their way to scatter Mrs. Huber's ashes, Edie interrogated Susan about her motives for tagging along. She assumed, correctly, that Susan had an ulterior motive, and told her, "You're still the perky cheerleader who thinks she can pull the wool over everyone's eyes." She also identified herself as the outsider in high school, who hung out with the "freaks on the loading dock and smoked," a status she recognizes—but doesn't necessarily completely embrace—as still hers in the present day on Wisteria Lane. In fact, her price for remaining silent about Susan's adventure in arson was an invitation to the Housewives' weekly poker game, along with the recognition that her presence may not be welcome. "I'm not saying your little friends have to be nice to me. But it would be nice just to be asked" ("Every Day a Little Death," 1–12).

This episode marked, in part, a turning point in the series for Susan and Edie. Freed from her own "secret," Susan could pursue the search for the truth behind Mary Alice's death. Except, for Susan, the search was no longer about Mary Alice at all, but instead about discovering how her lover Mike might or might not be involved. The shift in Susan's investment, from a jointly shared quest to a singularly held desire, signaled the ultimately heterosexual privileging of the text and narrowed the thematic point of view from the four Housewives to single housewife Susan. Susan's pursuit of her heterosexual happily ever after—which the other housewives had already achieved, more or less—was threatened by Mike's secrets, and so Susan became the truth-seeker in the text. This new alignment of Susan with truth was in part to reestablish the legitimacy of traditional values that had been called into question throughout the season by her doppelganger, Edie.

The text, however, continued to maintain the tension between the women by consciously *not* altering Edie's association with the truth. Indeed, she was the one who staged the "intervention" that questioned Susan's dogged loyalty to Mike. Thus, by her continued presence, her character works to subvert Susan's prominence and to interrogate the values that Susan embodies within the text.

The first season of *Desperate Housewives* ended with Edie's character still as much a work-in-progress as her unfinished house. But throughout the season her insistence on self-definition, as an outsider in the insider's world of Wisteria Lane, invited both viewers and readings contrary to the show's ostensible intentions. Edie's blunt, acerbic remarks are an alternative commentary on the goings-on of Wisteria Lane and a direct challenge to Mary Alice's heavenly sanctioned voice. Her performance of femininity, her control and recognition of her "excessive" sexuality and her continual focus on Susan continue the process, further destabilizing heterosexual values in service of a text that asks the question, "Who exactly is the girl next door?"

References

Carr, Kevin, "Desperate Housewives," 7MM Pictures, 2004.

Cherry, Marc, "Commentary: Pilot," *Desperate Housewives: The Complete First Season*, Buena Vista Television, 2005.

Kolodny, Annette, "A Map for Rereading: Gender and the Interpretation of Literary Texts," in *The New Feminist Criticism*, ed: Elaine Showalter. New York: Random House, 1985.

Mixon, Veronica, "Desperate Housewives," *Film Gazette*, 2004.

Mulvey, Laura, "Visual Pleasure and Narrative Cinema," in *Visual and Other Pleasures,* Bloomington, IN: Indiana University Press, 1989.

Parker, Tyler, "The Garbo Image," quoted in Esther Newton, *Mother Camp*. Chicago: University of Chicago Press, 1979.

Place, Janey, "Women in Film Noir" in *Women in Film Noir*, 1st edition. London: British Film Institute, 1978.

Plath, James, "Desperate Housewives," Reel.com, 2004.

Rich, B. Ruby, "She Says, He Says: The Power of the Narrator in Modernist Film Politics," in *Chick Flicks*. Durham, NC: Duke University Press, 1998.

Sontag, Susan, "Notes on Camp," in *Against Interpretation and Other Essays*. New York: Picador, 2001.

Sharon Bowers is an independent scholar who is interested in the intersections of gender, narrative and popular culture. She has presented at national and regional pop culture conferences on texts such as *ER*, *Fastlane* and *The L-Word*. The author of the novel *Lucifer Rising*, and a contributor to the *NYPD Blue* anthology *What Would Sipowicz Do?* she is currently working on a book-length examination of competitive discourses of sexuality in primetime television.

As someone who considers herself a free-floating signifier, she admires Edie's interrogative potential (if not her fashion sense) but wishes she had Bree's proficiency with a handgun (not to mention a basket of her muffins).

Shanna Swendson

A Morality Play
for the Twenty-First Century

The memorable last scene of the Desperate Housewives
*credits drops the show's stars into an Adam and Eve paint-
ing by early sixteenth-century painter Lucas Cranach the
Elder. That—and Carlos' occasional attempts at control-
ling Gabrielle—isn't the only thing that borders on medieval about* Desperate Housewives; *the show itself, the
interactions of its characters, functions like a morality
play straight out of the middle ages. Shanna Swendson explains.*

*I*N MEDIEVAL TIMES, church leaders used morality plays to
provide instruction to the largely illiterate populace. These
plays created characters out of vices and virtues, exaggerating their
traits so audiences could fully grasp their respective folly and wisdom.
By seeing the impact of these traits on the life of the "Everyman" character, audiences knew better how to live their own lives, which virtues
to strive for and which vices to avoid.

In the twenty-first century, we watch *Desperate Housewives.*

Our society isn't nearly as illiterate, nor does it look for the same
kind of instruction from entertainment as in medieval times, but there's
still an unbroken line between the morality plays of the medieval era
and *Desperate Housewives.* Morality plays grew out of the miracle plays,
which depicted biblical characters and lives of the saints. While the mo-

rality plays focused on similar spiritual themes, they presented their message using secular characters who might interact with characters representing virtues and vices. From the morality plays, secular theater evolved, still presenting the essential conflict of good against evil in the human soul, but with less overt religious doctrine. As technology changed, theater developed into motion pictures, radio and television dramas, all giving us characters against which we can measure and evaluate our own lives as they struggle with the questions of good, evil and everything in between. And that brings us to Wisteria Lane.

The housewives on Wisteria Lane offer a cast of anthropomorphized virtues and vices as clear as those depicted in any medieval morality play. However, modern times are a lot more complicated and full of gray areas. No single church or religious ideology is in a position to hold sway over an entire population, so there are differences of opinion as to what's a virtue and what's a vice. With the moral relativism of our time, virtues like Knowledge, Strength, Good Deeds and Truth aren't so black and white. Neither are vices like Flesh, Lust, Gluttony and Wrath. Where does motive fit in? What if a good deed is done from impure motivation, or a deed meant for good has evil consequences? Modern people recognize that there are often vices within virtues, and even virtues within vices.

We've also heard plenty about all of these virtues and vices. We know Greed and Lust are generally negative and Truth and Mercy are generally good. But what about other virtues and vices that may not be as major in a spiritual sense, but can wreak just as much havoc on our lives? Medieval people locked in a desperate battle for day-to-day survival probably didn't have to worry much about balancing work and family life. Without cell phones and answering machines, drunk dialing and ex-stalking wouldn't have been much of an issue. No indoor plumbing meant a shiny bathroom floor wasn't a major concern. Things like Stress and Perfectionism may be the kind of vices we need to be instructed on in our times.

Instead of watching Envy and Good Deeds slug it out on the front steps of a church, we watch the dangers of Impulsiveness and Self-Indulgence on television every Sunday night.

Let's meet our characters in today's version of a morality play:

Susan—Impulsiveness

SUSAN: You want humiliation, I'll give you humiliation. I locked myself
    out of my house, stark naked, and got caught by Mike.
GABRIELLE: Oh my God, when did this happen?
SUSAN: Today. Right before the party.
MIKE: What can I say? Right place, right time! ("Pretty Little Picture,"
    1–3)

Impulsiveness doesn't usually show up on the more common lists of
sins, but in the *Desperate Housewives* morality play, it's the sin that seems
to get the swiftest punishment. Susan leads with her heart, saying and
doing things the moment they occur to her, and she's usually reaping
the consequences of her impulse by the time her brain catches up. The
result is one disaster after another. She can't seem to get away with anything. Any little slip-up lands her in the kind of worst-case scenario situation most of us only imagine in our worst nightmares. She's a walking
test case for Murphy's Law. If something can go wrong for Susan, it will,
and usually quite spectacularly.

Most of us have worried about getting locked out of our homes by
being careless and forgetting our keys. It's happened to many of us
(though in my case, the door was actually unlocked, but the doorknob
refused to work—try telling a neighbor you're locked out of your house
when you're holding your house keys). That fear helps keep us from
forgetting our keys, or otherwise rushing out of the house unprepared
to face the world. But how many of us have managed to get locked out
of the house stark naked? Susan did, thanks to the impulse to confront
her ex-husband while she was wearing nothing more than a towel. To
make matters worse, the man she was trying to snare came by at the
worst possible moment, catching her stuck naked in the bushes. She's
toppled precariously balanced wedding cakes, gotten knocked out by
mechanical bulls and generally goes through life in one big pratfall. If
you've imagined a form of public humiliation, Susan has probably experienced it, and usually because of some seemingly inconsequential decision she's made.

When we do something that we know we probably shouldn't be doing, we may worry about doing something stupid that gets us caught. In
fact, that worry is often what prevents us from doing things we shouldn't
or going places where we shouldn't be. Worst-case scenarios usually
don't come to pass, often because of that little fearful warning in our
brains. But not for Susan. She might not have been caught while snoop-

ing on Edie to see if Mike was at Edie's house, but she accidentally set the house on fire, then wound up being blackmailed by a nosy neighbor and then tormented by Edie when the truth finally came out. If the imagined worst-case scenario in that particular situation is being caught and embarrassed, Susan's results go well beyond that.

Just about every impulse Susan acts on backfires on her, from almost killing Mike's dog with one of her earrings when her plan to make the dog like her goes awry, to getting caught prying into Mike's affairs when the bathroom floor gives way under her, leaving her stranded with the evidence visible. It's as though Susan lacks that "what could go wrong?" filter in her brain. She also tends to overlook whether or not it is the right moment to deal with an issue. If she wants to talk about something, she brings it up without thinking about the time or place. If she's curious about her mysterious father, she'll ask her mother even as they walk down the aisle during a wedding rehearsal.

Because of this, even her attempts to do the right thing have unintended consequences, such as when she ended up sabotaging her daughter's musical performance by coming clean about her motivations in edging Edie out of the way, or when she admitted her unintended arson to Edie at a very bad moment. Her life is a constant no-win situation. Whether she does the right thing or the wrong thing, it's guaranteed to end badly.

Susan's string of disasters teaches us that thinking first, before acting or talking, can help us avoid problems.

Lynette—Stress

LAUREN: Look, all I can tell you is plan ahead next time.

LYNETTE: Uh, Lauren? I'm a mother of four. Today I had to get up at five, make lunches, make breakfast, drop the twins off at school, and get across town lugging a baby and a sick child. Telling me to plan ahead is like telling me to sprout wings. And it's things like being told to plan ahead that make me so crazy that yoga is the only thing that relaxes me, except I show up here, and I can't get in, and you tell me to plan ahead. It's a vicious cycle. See how that works? ("Every Day a Little Death," 1–12)

Stress is such a part of everyday life for most modern women that today's fiction might as well make Stress a regular character. In *Desperate Housewives*, Lynette is that character. Family or career? Either way, you're bound to end up feeling in over your head at some point in time.

With family, friends, job, home, community and other responsibilities, there are a lot of balls to keep in the air, and Lynette's story is all about how hard it is to juggle.

Lynette left the stressful, busy world of a high-powered business-woman, only to find out that managing three young boys and a baby, as well as a rather boyish husband, is more challenging than managing an entire staff of professionals. While keeping the household running, she desperately struggles to keep up with her own expectations of what it means to be a wife and mother—not to mention what she sees as the expectations of everyone around her—all while trying not to lose track of her own identity.

Sometimes that juggling act leads her to acts of desperation, such as abandoning her misbehaving boys on the side of a road—just for a moment—to teach them a lesson or taking her sons' Ritalin to keep herself going when she has too much to get done and not enough hours in the day.

But it's not really being a mother that overwhelms Lynette and causes her stress. When she returns to the corporate world and leaves her husband at home with the children, she's just as flustered and juggling just as many balls. She has a hard time leaving any of her mom duties behind, even though she's taken on new responsibilities outside the home. You have to wonder if she actually kind of likes being that stressed—if stress and demands make her feel valued and important. If there's no stress, that could mean she's not needed. We saw that when she hired a nanny to help ease her burden, and then quickly became dissatisfied with not feeling as needed. Whenever her life starts to become easier, she manages to find a way to make things difficult again. Her competitive streak leads her to take on additional responsibilities, and her disciplinary methods seem almost designed to ensure that her boys will be hard to handle. Before she left the workplace to have children, she was probably the kind of person who changed her mind about a project at the last second because she loved the rush of pulling an all-nighter to get the project done on time, and she likely bragged often about how many hours she put in at the office (I've worked with a Lynette or two in the past).

We learn from Lynette that whether we choose career, or family, or some blend of the two, we're probably going to feel overwhelmed at times. We also learn that sometimes we bring that stress on ourselves, and even like it. Being overwhelmed by demands means a lot of people need you. Lynette's overload actually gives her a sense of power, and taking that into consideration makes us re-evaluate the stress in our own lives.

Bree—Perfection

DANIELLE: Daddy says he's having a heart attack.
BREE: I know. I'm going to take him to the hospital.
DANIELLE: Well, when?
BREE: When I finish making the bed.
DANIELLE: What?
BREE: I never leave the house with an unmade bed. You know that.
   ("Goodbye For Now," 1–22)

Never a hair out of place, never a speck of dust visible, gourmet meals on the table every night and a spotless kitchen: That's a life most of us can only dream about. But for Bree, the living embodiment of the virtue of Perfection, it's all in a day's work. She can throw a perfect dinner party without breaking a sweat, is there with home-baked muffins to welcome a new neighbor even on the day of her husband's death and has the best lawn on the block.

There's a sense about Bree that if she can control her surroundings into perfection, everything else will fall right into place. I'd be happy with just the tiniest fraction of her flawlessness—I don't even manage to make the bed on most mornings, let alone before I leave to take someone to the emergency room with a heart attack. (Though I think I did make my bed before going to the emergency room when I thought I had appendicitis because I knew if I were hospitalized, people might have to get into my home to bring me things. Maybe Bree has a point.) Being able to open the front door to another person without worrying about them seeing my cluttered living room would be nice, even if I'm not co-ordinated enough to invite people over for dinner.

But is that kind of perfection really a virtue? Bree's story shows us that, perhaps, she actually represents the vice of Control. Her perfection is a veneer. Under the surface, her life is as mixed up as anyone else's, if not more so. Her children are rebelling, her son is a budding sociopath with one death (so far) on his record, her husband resented her control and perfection so much that he wanted a divorce and saw a dominatrix (the kind in black leather with a whip, not the kind in pearls and a pastel twin set) on the side and she makes poor decisions about some of the people she trusts, such as pharmacist George.

The more she grasps at control, the more out-of-control her life becomes. Would she have had so many problems with Rex and her children if she'd let them eat macaroni and cheese made from a box every so often instead of serving a carefully crafted gourmet meal every night, or if she'd let them try—and even fail—at some task on their own? Not that all of her problems were strictly her fault, but for those of us for whom perfection is unreachable, it's nice to know that being perfect doesn't necessarily make for a perfect life.

Gabrielle—Self-Indulgence

GABRIELLE: I feel trapped.

JOHN: You want me to open a window?

GABRIELLE: No, I'm talking about my life.

JOHN: Oh. Are we done making out?

GABRIELLE: No, no. Keep going.

JOHN: So what's up?

GABRIELLE: I'm unhappy with Carlos and my marriage. I feel like I don't have options, and it's driving me crazy. Every time something went south in my life, I always had a Plan B. Now I feel like I have nothing.

JOHN: What about me? Can't I be your Plan B?

GABRIELLE: Damn it, John. What is our new rule?

JOHN: Stop pretending we have a future.

GABRIELLE: Thank you. ("Live Alone and Like It," 1–19)

There's a little bit of princess in just about every woman, and Gabrielle reflects this desire for adoration and lots of pretty things. She embodies the vice of Self-Indulgence, and her story shows just how damaging this vice can be when taken to extremes. She has snared the dream husband—a rich man who is crazy about her. She has a fabulous house, a beautiful wardrobe, expensive jewelry and hot new cars. And when that wasn't enough for her, when her husband was too busy earning money (to buy her things) to lavish her with personal attention, she found another man who adored her even more than her husband did, her hot teenage gardener. Young John couldn't buy her all the things she wants (one shopping spree was enough to raise fraud flags on his credit card), but he could give her a single perfect rose and all the ardor of youthful adoration. When both of these relationships were working for her, Gabrielle had the best of both worlds. She had a rich man to shower her with gifts and a devoted boy to shower her with affection. If she isn't getting what she wants, whether materially or emotionally, she has no qualms about demanding it because she feels she deserves it.

In the hints of Gabrielle's background we've been given, we understand that she once was poor, that she pulled herself up out of that and made a life for herself, and is now determined never to go back. Her story is like watching what happens after the happily ever after, once Cinderella has found her handsome prince. Will the scullery maid ever be comfortable in the castle, or will she live in fear of having to shed the glass slippers and go back to the ashes?

No matter how much we have, there are times when we want more—more clothes, more shoes, more *things*, more love. Gabrielle serves as an object lesson on the dangers inherent in chronic dissatisfaction. She hurts those around her, and even sometimes sabotages herself, in her ongoing quest for fulfillment. If only she would realize that she'll never be truly happy if she continues to look to other people and things to fill her inner emptiness rather than looking inside herself.

For those of us who aren't princesses living in modern-day castles, and who don't have men fighting over us, it's occasionally nice to see that having those things doesn't necessarily make anyone happy in the long term. As overwhelmed as Lynette is, she probably has more personal satisfaction in her life than Gabrielle does. She has a husband who is truly a partner in her life and children who may drive her crazy, but who love her. Gabrielle has beautiful things that are far too easy to lose when the creditors show up.

Those glass slippers really don't look too comfortable, do they?

Edie—Candor

EDIE: She's upset with Mike, isn't she? Well, come on. I'm gonna find out sooner or later.

LYNETTE: She's devastated about the breakup, and she hasn't left the house in days.

EDIE: Well, why didn't you just tell me that?

LYNETTE: Because it's personal. It's the kind of thing she would only want me to tell her friends.

EDIE: I'm Susan's friend. Well, I don't hate her.

LYNETTE: Edie, if you want me to share stuff with you, you're gonna have to start being more supportive of Susan.

EDIE: Okay. How?

LYNETTE: What do friends do? They call, they're sympathetic, they ask about the pain the other person is going through, and then they listen.

EDIE: What if you want to be supportive, but you just can't stand listening to people bitch? ("The Ladies Who Lunch," 1–16)

Sometimes, traits that look virtuous may hide a vice, and traits that look like vices can be virtues in disguise. Edie may be cast as the villain of Wisteria Lane, but in many ways, the trait of candor she embodies can be a virtue. Every so often, wouldn't it be nice to be able to ignore the conventions of society, to stop worrying about what other people think and just do what you want, to go after anyone you desired in a no-holds-barred way? That's the way Edie lives. She's utterly shameless in her flirting techniques and her wardrobe, in the things she says to her neighbors and in her pursuit of men. She'll stop at nothing to get what she wants. If she makes some enemies along the way, well, those weren't people she wanted as friends anyway. It's a life lived in near-total honesty, both with herself and with others, and she's probably caused less pain to others in her life than any of the other housewives.

If Edie got herself into the kinds of mishaps Susan does, you can imagine she'd handle them in an entirely different way—if she even got into those mishaps in the first place. She'd have no shame about being seen naked outside her home and probably would have walked right up to someone's door and rung the bell to ask for help. She'd have bluntly asked Mike what he was hiding if she found guns and cash in his kitchen instead of sneaking around to snoop behind his back (and ending up falling through the floor). She has the kind of confidence with men that says she's more concerned about whether she should like them than about whether they like her.

Unlike her neighbors, Edie doesn't really have anything to hide (that we know of so far). If she has a grudge against someone, she's already told them. If she's done something wrong, she probably did it openly and in public. She's not covering up a murder or a manslaughter and she doesn't have anyone chained in the basement, so she doesn't have much to lie about. She is what she is, take her or leave her.

She may be as selfish as Gabrielle, but she seems to be more satisfied with her life. She doesn't feel trapped. If she isn't getting what she wants, she'll go after it herself instead of finding someone to get it for her. She's not exactly a role model, and I wouldn't advocate making "What would Edie do?" a personal mantra, but the woman does have guts—and, perhaps most importantly, the guts to be honest. The more timid among us could stand to learn a thing or two from her.

Although the medieval morality plays may seem simplistic in their depiction of virtues and vices, their technique is an effective one, making traits larger than life so they can be fully examined. Impulsiveness, Stress, Perfection (or Control), Self-Indulgence and Candor are all "characters" we see in our day-to-day lives. Perhaps by putting a face on them and laughing (or crying) with them on Sunday evenings, we can all learn a little something about how these virtues and vices affect us, as well as learning what to do—or what not to do—when we face them in our own lives.

Shanna Swendson is neither a housewife nor desperate (though she probably needs to get out more often). She is the critically acclaimed author of the novel *Enchanted, Inc.* and its sequel, *Once Upon Stilettos*, and she was a contributor to *Flirting With Pride and Prejudice*. If she had to pick the Desperate Housewife she's most like, it would be Susan, though she was fully clothed the last time she got locked out of her house, her neighborhood is suffering a serious shortage of handsome plumbers and she seldom has a problem with impulse control.

Oh, Give Me a Home
Deconstructing the Houses of
Desperate Housewives

A woman's house is her domain, and according to Nancy Herkness, it gives away more of who she is, and what she values, than she would ever guess. From the façade of the front door to the id of the basement, a housewife's home, not her eyes, is the window to her soul.

AH, WISTERIA LANE: the model of a suburban street with its well-manicured lawns, white picket fences and impossibly beautiful houses without a single leaky gutter or flake of peeling paint. Of course, the contrast between the pristine façades and the dark secrets of the Desperate Housewives—and husbands—inhabiting them is exactly what the show's creators are after. As Thomas A. Walsh, the production designer, has said in the feature "Secrets of Wisteria Lane": "Part of our conceptual approach from the beginning was everything was a little heightened, everything was a little too perfect."

In reality, these are the façades of Universal Studios' "Colonial Street," previously home to families as widely disparate as the Cleavers and the Munsters. Now inhabited by the housewives of television's wildly popular nighttime soap opera, the too-perfect surfaces of these houses remind one of the sinister town of Stepford and the question Bree Van De Kamp poses in "Ah, But Underneath" (1–2): How much do we really want to know about our neighbors?

The answer, of course, is, "Everything!" As we drive around the streets of our suburban neighborhoods, we can't help speculating on what goes on behind the closed doors of these superficially serene, handsome homes.

Desperate Housewives invites us to come inside.

As we pass through the front doors, let's take a look at these dividers of the public and the private. Bree Van De Kamp's door is solid, with no windows to peek through. A quintessential WASP, she's obsessed with outward appearances; even when she gardens or washes dishes, she's perfectly color-coordinated and accessorized down to her work gloves. Bree's door says she doesn't want any neighbors finding a chink in her walls through which to examine the flaws in her family's lives. It's the door of someone who's private to the point of repression.

Gabrielle Solis, on the other hand, has a front door made almost entirely of panes of glass. There are no curtains, sheer or otherwise, to block the spectator's view. This is the door of a risk-taker, an exhibitionist, someone who does not draw a line between her public and her private personas. The former runway model wants people to watch her, no matter what she's doing. She craves an audience. Even her closet doors are glass, something no normal human being would dream of having since all the messes we hide would be exposed for the casual visitor to gape at.

Lynette Scavo and Susan Mayer's front doors fall somewhere between the two extremes. Lynette's door has a full-length glass inset but she covers it with tightly gathered sheer curtains. Light comes in and out, creating the illusion of openness, but, in fact, the curtains blur outlines and hide flaws. The stay-at-home mom who goes back to work, Lynette is frank to the point of rudeness but knows there's a difference between what should be public knowledge and what should remain private.

Susan's door is half-and-half: half wood, half glass, with a covering of sheer curtains. She's the "Everywoman" character, a typical suburbanite, so her door is average as well. Being the drama queen who is least competent in practical matters, Susan leaves the least imprint on her home, and her front door reflects this, waffling a bit between revealing and concealing.

Interestingly, her door resembles the handsome plumber Mike Delfino's, although he covers his glass panes with very manly plaid curtains that are more concealing than Susan's sheers. Are the show's designers hinting on a subliminal level that Mike and Susan are meant to be together? In truth, Mike is trying to create the illusion that he fits into the neighborhood, that he's just a regular guy, not a killer and a drug dealer who first moved there to spy on his neighbors and track down a murderer.

Notice the darkness of Mary Alice and Paul Young's door, the only one on the street which is painted black, the color that always signifies the bad guy (except in New York where everyone wears black). The entrance speaks of "the black night of the soul," of murder, suicide and madness. How much more clearly could the house say that to step through this portal is to step into a place of evil?

The façades of Wisteria Lane deliberately conceal the drama of the lives going on behind them. Their bland perfection is meant to provide a stark contrast to the life-altering disasters taking place behind those closed front doors, reminding us that surfaces are often untrustworthy and that surprises lie within both the houses and the characters who live there. Mr. Walsh and his colleagues toy with our expectations, using the façades to lull us into complacency, hinting at differences with the entrance doors, and finally giving us a revelation of individuality with the carefully chosen décor of the interiors.

After all, our homes are our castles, our sanctuaries, our showplaces and, most importantly, the stages on which we play out the private dramas of our lives. They reveal more about our personalities than we might be aware of, and Mr. Walsh uses the visual environment to tell us volumes about the Desperate Housewives without speaking a word.

Pass through the front door of Gabby and Carlos' house and your nostrils will fill with the smell of "new money." Not only do they decorate with hand-carved Italian tables, they know exactly how much the tables cost and will share the purchase price with their guests. The Solis household does not have curtains, it has window treatments: yards and yards of high-priced fabric draped in elaborate swags designed to call attention to themselves, not cover the windows. The house is a showplace where Carlos displays his beautiful wife in expensive surroundings.

For Gabby, the house is something she earned with grit, guts and good planning. She decided to haul herself up by her own bootstraps, and the house proves to her and the world how far she's come. The first thing she bought with the money she earned from modeling was the Renaissance painting of a Madonna and child in an ornate gilt frame which hangs over her fireplace. Old Masters and gold have always appealed to social climbers; they seem to confer legitimacy through their antiquity and extravagance. However, Gabby's own face decorates the staircase in a series of large Warhol-like silk screens. Warhol's style is so widely imitated that it has become almost a cliché of self-aggrandizement and, of course, he's famous for admitting that he didn't create all of the art to which he signed his name. So the Warhol portraits seem to interject doubt about Gabby and Carlos' acumen and genuineness.

Lynette's home, while generally in a state of chaos, is an open, airy, unpretentious family house. Kitchen, dining area and living room all run into each other with no demarcation. This is a place where children are welcome—perhaps too much so—in the public spaces. Overwhelmed by and often resentful of her job as a mother and housewife, Lynette hasn't learned to set boundaries for her children, so her house lacks them as well. Even the artwork runs to children's drawings magnetically attached to the refrigerator. Everything is there for the visitor to see but, unlike Gabby's, the display is not meant to impress; it's meant to disarm with frankness. Lynette's no-nonsense, take-me-as-I-am persona allows her to make brutally honest, often tactless comments which would be far more offensive if, say, Bree uttered them. Her house takes the same approach, saying, "Ignore the mess and enjoy me for the functional, warm place that I am."

The one person who can out-Martha Martha Stewart is, of course, Bree. Her home stands at the opposite pole from both Gabby and Lynette's. Immaculately neat, tastefully subtle, it whispers audibly that a control freak lives here. The rooms are all decorated in beige, taupe and cream. The floors are polished hardwood with an occasional area rug to break up the gleaming expanse. The emphasis is not on ostentation or warmth, but on understatement and good taste, the marks of "old money." Everything looks as though it was inherited from Bree or Rex's parents, or eccentric Aunt Bitsy whose great-great-grandmother came over on the Mayflower. Not a throw pillow is ever out of place and the silver gleams without a speck of tarnish.

Indeed, one of the most disturbing episodes of the first season occurred when Zach, the troubled adopted son of Mary Alice and Paul Young, broke into and decorated Bree's house for Christmas. He took over this perfectly controlled environment and imposed his own garish décor. Somehow this indicated his unstable mental state more clearly even than holding Susan at gunpoint in her kitchen, because it seemed much more bizarre and invasive.

Bree's choice of artwork becomes part of the story as the camera pans her walls. Mary Alice, in her role as narrator, explained that the foundation of Bree's life is expressed in the portraits of Jesus (faith in God), Ronald Reagan (love of country) and her family (love of family). Family is clearly the most important of those since she hangs that portrait over the fireplace, or hearth, signifying that it is the heart of her home. Of course, that is the part of her life that disintegrated over the course of the first season, as Andrew became a monster and Rex sickened and finally died, explaining why her desperation runs so deep.

Susan's house is the least idiosyncratic of all the abodes on Wisteria Lane. Considering the fact that she is an artist, one would expect more flair and style in her décor. She has one interesting collage hanging in her living room but it's not central to the scheme and one barely notices it. Her house seems smaller and a bit darker and more cramped than the other housewives', which may indicate her economic standing in the neighborhood as a single working mother. It also indicates Susan's immature approach to life; she is unwilling to step into the role of adult either in her relationship with her daughter, Julie, or in her own home. (Even her job keeps her infantilized to a certain extent; she illustrates children's books.) Like a child, she does not impose her identity on her environment. Her victim mentality and weak sense of self show in the haphazard, unremarkable interior of her home.

In contrast, Mike, the only man on Wisteria Lane with a house of his own, imprints his masculine persona strongly on his residence. From the rough-spun green plaid curtains on his front door to the deer antler lying on the side table in the sitting room, this house reeks of the ubermale. His fireplace is a heavy Roman arch of brick. His kitchen has solid, bead-board cabinets (where he hid a gun and stacks of money). A model of a sailing ship hints at Mike's darker side, evoking pirates and adventure on the high seas. There is no question that a man's man lives here. No wonder the unattached housewives swarmed to him like moths to a flame; even without that sculpted jaw and those piercing blue eyes, his virility would have been clear in his home decorating.

Martha Huber was marked for death by her house—"the place where good taste goes to die," as her sister Felicia remarked ("Children Will Listen," 1–18). No one with cheap china figurines on glass shelves and dowdy braided rugs (one of which Paul Young used to wrap up Martha's body after he murdered her) can be allowed to mar the perfection of Wisteria Lane for long. The ugliness of her surroundings reflects the ugliness of her soul. The viewer didn't need ominous music or careful foreshadowing to know that this woman was doomed; the set designers had already warned us by giving her a dreadful sense of aesthetics. A busybody whose blackmailing precipitated Mary Alice's suicide, Martha was never a sympathetic character. Even when she took Edie Britt in after her house burned down—a seemingly generous gesture—Martha stole Edie's jewelry. The evident shabbiness and lack of updating in Martha's home also underscored her reason for blackmailing Mary Alice: she needed the money.

If décor heightens character, consider the rooms each Housewife seems to spend the most time inhabiting. These preferences add yet another facet to their personalities.

Bree, for instance, chooses the dining room not just for meals and entertaining but for serious family meetings. This is the place where she reigns supreme because there is so much she can control. She sets the mood through the table settings, changing the lighting, the colors and the level of formality. She chooses the menu and prepares the food, allowing her to direct her family's health and tastes. She even keeps her Bible in a drawer of the sideboard, exerting a subtle spiritual influence. It's a public room where Bree can fully display her prowess in all matters domestic, the place where she feels the most powerful.

Susan, on the other hand, prefers the informality of her kitchen table. She doesn't necessarily do a great deal of food preparation there, since she's no more competent at cooking than at running the rest of her life. It's more a social center for her, a place to drink coffee and talk. She even works at the kitchen table, the same place a child often chooses to do homework. Susan wants to be in the midst of bustle rather than concentrating in private when she is performing her obligatory tasks. In fact, her daughter Julie also does homework at the kitchen table, and it was there Susan caught her kissing Zach, an indication of how innocent the relationship truly was. Zach had been in Julie's bedroom but they never kissed there; it would have been too dangerous. The kitchen table speaks of family and wholesomeness.

Lynette also enjoys being in the midst of her family. When she has a moment to relax, she gravitates toward the couch in her great room. It's an insane place to try to take a nap—or to seduce her husband in a French maid's costume, as she attempted to do in one episode—but it's the one she consistently chooses. Lynette lives her life in the open; she prides herself on being plain-spoken and honest. She needs to have her finger on the pulse of what's happening in her world all the time. She can't always control it but she needs to be central to it, and the great room couch gives her that position.

Some would argue that Gabby has spent most of her time in the bedroom, whether with Carlos or John the gardener, but the room where she's most relaxed and which best reflects her character is the marble-lined bathroom with its enormous sybaritic tub for two, giant mirror and flat-screen television set. The bathroom speaks of Gabby's sensuality and vanity as well as her taste for ostentation. Although this is usually the most private of rooms, Gabby has happily invited both her husband and lover in (although not simultaneously), lolling decadently amongst the soapsuds with them. She even pulls the outside world in by hanging a television set on the wall. It gives her the illusion of having an audience. And it gives the cable guy the opportunity to slip on the wet marble.

The episode with the hapless cable repairman highlights the show's highly effective and humorous use of visual shorthand. Erroneously convinced that Gabby was sleeping with the cable guy, Carlos burst into the poor fellow's apartment and began to beat him. As he was standing over his battered victim, his (and the camera's) eye focused on a poster for the musical *Gypsy*. Then he panned to two Robert Mapplethorpe-ish photographs of bare male chests. Finally, he zoomed in on a framed snapshot of the cable guy embracing another man. Without a single word being spoken, we and Carlos simultaneously realized the repairman was gay. Although of course we already knew Carlos had the wrong man, how much funnier was it to show Carlos as being so utterly off-base? Not to mention that the "gay-bashing" thread was used to embroider Carlos' crimes as the season progressed.

As the house manifests character, it also displays status. When Carlos got into legal and financial difficulties, the one thing he and Gabby did not want to do was sell the house. Why? Because it's the most substantial symbol of their success. To have a home means one is a person of means. Losing it is the ultimate failure. In the final crisis, Gabby persuaded Carlos that it was better to go to jail for eight months than to give up the home they'd both worked so hard to acquire. The same house they treasure also became something of an albatross around their necks, with hilarious results. When the main sewage pipe clogged and they couldn't afford to repair it, they did their laundry in the backyard jacuzzi. In desperation, Gabby stole a port-a-potty from a construction site so she wouldn't have to think up new excuses to use her neighbor's bathrooms.

Of course, a home can be a prison as well. Carlos' home became his jail when he was under house arrest. His ankle bracelet notified the police if he strayed beyond the confines of his yard. Gabby reminded him of his restricted life when she took a bucket of fried chicken and retreated across the street to savor it alone as Carlos growled with hunger. And Caleb was held in chains in newcomer Betty Applewhite's basement, a prison in the most literal sense.

The house also functions as a scapegoat. When Paul tried to persuade Zach to leave Wisteria Lane in an attempt to outrun their violent past, he claimed it was because the house was not healthy. Mike explained away the cuts and bruises he sported after being beaten by a crooked police officer by saying he fell down the stairs.

In power struggles, the home becomes a pawn. Gabby's overbearing mother-in-law established her supremacy right from the start by choosing the color the house was painted. When "Mama Solis" came to visit, Gabby was driven out of the house and onto her front porch to do her daily yoga. Susan's mother Sophie moved in after leaving her latest beau, and the mother and daughter battled over Sophie bringing men into the house.

If the house says so much, what does lack of a house indicate about a character? Edie became homeless when Susan accidentally (or not?) set fire to her house by knocking a burning candle into her curtains. Cast as the dangerous vamp of the neighborhood, the one who might tempt the other housewives' husbands to stray, Edie's lack of a house made her even more dangerous; she needed a new nest and she might have set her sights on yours.

Ironically, Edie deals in houses. As she said in "The Ladies Who Lunch" (1–16), "Of course I believe in evil. I work in real estate." She put up the "For Sale" sign on Paul Young's house—and took it down when Zach refused to leave. She sold the house to Betty Applewhite. And she often has access to houses when the owners are not there, giving her the opportunity to uncover their secrets.

Yet Edie is ultimately a weak secondary character. Neither her strong sexuality nor her control over the all-important home gives her significant influence in the neighborhood. Perhaps this is because her impact is focused on the men of Wisteria Lane, and men are not the rulers here. The housewives wield the power in this world, and they neither like nor trust Edie. Of course, she recognized this and forced her way into their regular poker game, telling them they should invite her whether she chooses to attend or not. The Housewives came to tolerate her presence and even use her occasionally (for clandestine entrance into the Young's house, for advice on how to handle a rival, etc.). Their attitude toward her, however, is still ambivalent, as is hers toward them. She has yet to be admitted to the inner circle, partly because she's not sure she wants to be there.

Given that the set designers pay such close attention to detail, it is interesting to note some significant items these houses are missing. Considering the extraordinarily trim figures of all the characters, why is there not a treadmill or elliptical trainer anywhere in sight? Or a home office complete with computer and Internet access? Technology seems to have bypassed Wisteria Lane, perhaps because the show's creators wish to emphasize the timelessness of the human drama. And since electronics become obsolete as soon as the consumer gets them home, these accessories would quickly seem dated.

As anyone who lives in the suburbs can tell you, most houses have at least one contractor or painter or electrician's truck parked in front of them on a regular basis. Yet the Desperate Housewives never renovate. Only Mike did any obvious work on his home, gutting his upstairs bathroom (the one where Susan falls through the floor), presumably to spruce it up although we never see the finished room. Bree once wielded a paintbrush on her planters and Paul once touched up his picket fence. (Interestingly, both of them used white paint, leading one to muse upon the metaphorical aspects of white-washing, something both of them do a great deal of.) But major projects? They only happen when catastrophe strikes, as in the case of Edie's house burning down or Susan's kitchen exploding. And as Teri Hatcher observed in an interview, when Susan's kitchen was redone, they didn't even change the tile.

Until the second season, not a single basement appeared in these homes. Of course, one could argue that basements are traditionally the domain of husbands and children since they are often home to bars, pool tables and/or rec rooms. Perhaps that would explain the absent exercise equipment as well. But why do the show's creators never allow us to visit the foundations of their characters' houses? Did they decide to wait until the second season to reveal the more subterranean depths of the housewives' souls? Certainly Betty Applewhite finds a unique and deeply sinister use for her basement. Hopefully, in the future, we will be allowed more glimpses into the regular characters' dark underground recesses, their "ids."

Ultimately the unhinged pharmacist George Williams understood better than anyone else the pivotal role of the home in these housewives' world. His obsessive and murderous courtship of Bree culminated when he proposed to her, tempting her not with a ring (although he gave her one of those too) but with a new house. He comprehended how thoroughly the identities of the Desperate Housewives are wrapped up in and reflected by their homes. He grasped the significance of the roles of the house: status symbol, sanctuary, showplace and, most importantly, stage. After all, every housewife needs a place to strut and fret for her desperate hour.

References

"Secrets of Wisteria Lane." *Desperate Housewives: The Complete First Season.* Bonus Feature. ABC: 2005.

Nancy Herkness is the author of two award-winning novels: *A Bridge to Love* and *Shower of Stars*. She learned how to "deconstruct" at Princeton University, where she studied English literature and creative writing. Born and raised in the mountains of West Virginia, Nancy now lives in New Jersey with her husband, two children and a golden retriever. She was shocked to discover that, according to the *Desperate Housewives* Quiz, she most resembles the character of Gabrielle. Of course, she wouldn't mind having Gabby's figure or her shoes.

Deanna Carlyle

America the Superficial?
Watching *Desperate Housewives*
with the Europeans

At a time when anti-American sentiment is at an all-time high in the international arena, Desperate Housewives *has taken the world by storm. But are Europeans, Asians, Africans and Australians seeing the same thing we are when they turn on their television sets? Or, American-in-Stuttgart Deanna Carlyle asks, as with foreign voice dubbing, is something lost—or even gained—in translation?*

EUROPEANS LOVE—and often prefer—American cultural products like *Desperate Housewives.* Yet they have a hard time reconciling what they see on the screen with what they believe about Americans. In a recent screenwriting seminar I took in Stuttgart, for instance, I was intrigued by the curious mix of admiration and denigration the participants expressed about American movies and TV series. The German screenwriters simply could not figure out how an apparently facile nation of people—i.e., superficial, uneducated Americans—could produce such subtle, innovative and psychologically sophisticated cultural products like *Desperate Housewives.*

Why do Europeans erroneously assume Americans are superficial? What cross-cultural patterns underpin this assumption? Equally intriguing, why do Americans remain top competitors worldwide in the entertainment industry despite their supposed superficiality? And how is it that the very Europeans who assume Americans are superficial also experience deep meaning while watching *Desperate Housewives?*

As a desperate *Hausfrau* living in Europe, I decided to find out. Reader beware: I'll be using generalizations like "Europeans," "Germans," "the French" and "Americans." I'm referring to mainstream cultural norms. Subcultural patterns may vary. If you're an American, you're about to peer into the deepest crannies of your cultural identity. If you're a European, you're about to do the same. Fasten your seatbelts. This could be a bumpy ride.

Explicit vs. Implicit Culture

In an early episode of *Desperate Housewives* Susan's daughter Julie introduced herself to their new neighbor Mike. She was on a mission to find out as much as she could about her mother's potential love interest. And thanks to the explicit nature of American communication patterns, she had an easy time gathering good dirt. After her brief meeting with Mike, Julie reported back to her mom with more details than any European would ever have been able to find out about a neighbor in five minutes: Mike's wife died a year earlier. He'd wanted to stay in L.A., but left because of painful memories there. He was renting a house on Wisteria Lane for tax purposes, but hoped to buy a place soon.

On watching this scene, my German husband remarked that it was unrealistic and superficial of Mike to reveal so much about himself in so short a time. Mike barely knew Julie, so my German reasoned; only people who are good friends reveal so much about themselves up front. Not in my book, they don't. As an American, I come from what cross-cultural theorists call an explicit, or low-context, culture, where not only is it polite to lay most of your cards on the table right away, it's actually necessary for the smooth functioning of society. With so many successive waves of immigration, frontier-culture Americans can't assume that the new family on the block will share the same cultural values. The newcomer may worship a different god or no god at all, may speak a different language or hail from a region with an entirely different climate.

It follows that even if Americans never end up becoming bosom buddies with their new neighbors—and luckily for *Desperate Housewives* fans, Susan and Mike *did* become bosom buddies—both parties need to unpack their personal history right up front. This is the only way they can begin to find common ground. As a result, both old and new neighbors will have enough information to know whether or not to pursue the connection.

In other words, detailed American introductions like those found in *Desperate Housewives* are not superficial; they're practical.

Unlike Americans, Europeans have an implicit, or high-context, culture. They are accustomed to sharing a set of assumptions with their compatriots, so all they have to do is subtly refer to that common ground rather than explicitly stating their personal history. Of course, their behavior is changing slightly as Europeans become more mobile and international within EU borders, but because they still tend to relocate less often than Americans, they continue to act according to implicit cultural norms.

In other words, it's not that Europeans are cold or rude; they're just being efficient.

A pity that some Europeans mistake Americans' informative bent for hot air and superficial friendship. Consider this remark from a German *Desperate Housewives* fan I interviewed: "We Germans do welcome our neighbors too, but we don't do it in such a formalized, presentational way like on *Desperate Housewives*, as if showing off. To me, the cliché of an American is the show-off, someone who plays a role to get attention, but there's not any real content behind all the presentation.... Germans don't talk as much or as loudly. There's less chatter and filler in our conversation."

In other words, Germans are supposed to be deep, Americans shallow. So untrue!

Another supposed indicator of American superficiality is our explicit discussion of expenses and price tags. A European would never, for example, tell her young lover that she wants to make love on her dining room table because it cost her husband $23,000, as Gabrielle did in the pilot episode of *Desperate Housewives*. Nor would a European discuss his investments at a party, as Carlos did with his colleagues. For many Europeans this price awareness is a sign of American moral turpitude, as if by publicly discussing the price of our home or a recent purchase we automatically brand ourselves as less concerned with deeper human values.

Yet, in a low-context culture like that of the U.S., referring to an item's cost serves a positive, practical function. It immediately gives conversationalists much-needed information and a frame of reference. It's one more way of unpacking the suitcase so that others can know who and what they're dealing with and make decisions accordingly.

Europeans who criticize the "dollarization" of American values forget that status determination is a universally human instinct that serves the smooth functioning of the group (wolves and walruses do it too, and even more explicitly, at that). And while it's true that some personality types, like Carlos and Gabrielle's, are more focused on status symbols than others, it's equally true that all socialized humans seek a clear status in one form or another, be it through their expertise, income or social role. The French do it by subtly referencing their influence, their connections and their cultural knowledge. Same function, different factor.

Individuation vs. Fusion

In "Suspicious Minds" (1–9), Lynette's nanny sent the Scavo boys off with a wink and the imperative, "Have fun." Likewise, in a later episode their father Tom sent the boys outside, first making them promise to play alone for twenty minutes. This sort of childrearing practice is another root cause of European stereotypes about American superficiality.

American children are encouraged from an early age to separate from their caregivers and to explore their environment on their own. In contrast, children in more clan-based, traditional societies like Europe's are discouraged from straying too far afield. While an American mother and father will tell their kids, "You can do it," and "Go have fun," the way Tom and Lynette did, a French parent will say, "Don't go too far away, I want to be able to see you." And if the child then falls and hurts himself, or makes a mistake, the French parent will say, "I told you not to go too far." When an American child makes a mistake, on the other hand, or incurs a minor injury, his caregiver will matter-of-factly explain what happened, then send the child off with, "Try it again. You can do it."

Both nationalities are giving their children imperatives and unconscious messages. The French imperative is "Stay close, don't separate," which the French child interprets as, "I want you close to me," and sadly, "You are incompetent." In contrast, the American imperatives are "You must do it on your own," and "Go away and explore. Separate." The American child interprets these statements to mean, "You are capable," and sadly too, "I don't want you close to me."

Because Americans psychologically separate from their parents at an early age—while many Europeans never achieve individuation—they experience their body and their self, and even their thoughts, as separate from the environment. As a result, Americans can more easily create new mental categories. Witness the prolific technological and creative innovation so characteristic of American culture. To innovate, one must combine two or more previously existing phenomena to create an entirely new phenomenon. This particularly American bent is good not only for the American economy but also for America's image abroad, reinforcing positive stereotypes of Americans as optimistic, creative problem-solvers and innovators of cultural products like *Desperate Housewives*.

On the downside, the individuated American is lonelier than the more relational, clan-focused European, and more concerned that others should like him (based on an early unconscious sense of being unwanted). Hence the broad American smile, a permanent fixture on *Desperate Housewives* characters like Susan and Bree, their invitation to strangers to like them and be liked by them, to approve and be approved.

Unfortunately, Europeans misunderstand this American smile. They see it as either a sign of imbecility or a type of insincere commercial, as if Americans were trying to sell them something, perhaps through deception. Secure in their knowledge that they are wanted and loved by those close to them—if also smothered and discouraged to individuate—Europeans don't go out of their way to smile at strangers. After thousands of years of scarcity, rigid class structure and criticism from their parents, teachers and authority figures, Europeans are simply more fearful and pessimistic than Americans about the intentions of those outside the safety of their clan. They don't trust a stranger's smile; it might deprive them of their dignity or their money in a world where both are scarce.

To thrive in what they perceive as a hostile environment, Europeans focus on building fusional, clan-like relationships that grow outward from their family, school friends and lifelong colleagues. This is one reason they move less often from region to region and why they experience friendly, geographically mobile Americans—like the successive waves of new neighbors on Wisteria Lane—as superficial. Europeans don't understand that Americans experience themselves as individuated, as separate from a group—in it, but not of it. Less afraid of attack and criticism than Europeans and inured by early separation from their parents, Americans let down their guard. They are more willing to risk a smile, admit a weakness and reveal personal information.

Americans trust that wherever they go, their new neighborhood will provide a new support system, like the Neighborhood Watch program on *Desperate Housewives*, the babysitting that Lynette's neighbors provide for her and the furniture storage Bree offered Gabrielle. Europeans rarely receive such frontier-like support when they relocate. It's understood in Europe that either the State will watch out for you or your family will—and indeed both do a good job—not necessarily your neighbors.

Another misunderstanding about the individuated American concerns self-decoration and modification. The Europeans I interviewed consider American women—especially American actresses like Nicollette Sheridan who plays Edie—to be superficial because they wear more makeup, hair extensions and fake fingernails than their European counterparts. The same goes for the other actresses on *Desperate Housewives*, who've evidently had their eyelids done and who knows what else. Europeans—including European actors—are hesitant to tamper with their body like this, while Americans feel less threatened by extensions and modifications.

Susanne Moll, a German documentary filmmaker and *Desperate Housewives* fan, puts it this way: "The cliché of the American woman involves things like well-dressed, stylish ladies with perfect hair and makeup. I think a lot of German women tend to both envy and look down on American women who seem to be concentrating too much on their looks and appearance.... Same with the *Desperate Housewives* stars in every episode; they have special outfits and hairstyles. It's superficial, but we envy it too."

And yet American self-modification is not necessarily a sign of superficiality. It also betokens a strong sense of self. As individuated beings, cut off early from their caretakers and thrust into the world, Americans experience their self as slightly separate from their body. So it's no skin off their nose if they get a tattoo or a boob job. Their essential self remains unscathed.

In Europe, on the other hand, getting a tattoo or cosmetic surgery is akin to modifying your very being. Incompletely individuated as they are, Europeans experience more fusion between their body and their sense of self, in the same way that they experience more fusion between their identity and their various clans—with the result that they misinterpret American decoration on shows like *Desperate Housewives* as a sign of a shallow, inconstant inner being. Alas!

Verticality vs. Horizontality

In the U.S., even the layout of our cities mirrors our sense of individuation. Like the characters on Wisteria Lane, many Americans live in Suburbia, a decentralized place without a city center. Americans experience this social space from within a horizontal, decentralized orientation, not a vertical, centralized one as in Europe, where hierarchies are more rigid and power more centralized—the legacy of feudalism.

Europeans view this American horizontal orientation as superficial.

They assume that since Americans have no city center, they have no focus, no culture, no history, and thus no depth. As TV reporter and *Desperate Housewives* fan Ophelia Dittmann puts it, "German cities are more unique than American cities, less interchangeable," a comment which makes me smile as an American living in Germany. I have a hard time telling German cities apart.

In contrast to Americans, Europeans are more focused on their past, on the history and continuity of their various clans, each centered around a person, a city, a duchy, a nation and so on, and each ranked in hierarchical orientation vis-à-vis other clans. This is what cross-cultural theorists call a vertical orientation. As Joachim Geil, the German curator and screenwriter I interviewed, told me, "German cities arise around one or more historical city centers. They have an identity that revolves strongly around the past and its successive waves of outward growth."

In contrast, Americans with their suburban sprawl are present- and future-oriented as they move horizontally through American space into the future. This horizontal orientation makes Americans appear rudderless to Europeans. But because we Americans are more individuated, mobile and horizontally oriented, we each create our own sense of direction, our own trajectory through future space.

This horizontality is also visible in American social interactions, taking the form of politeness with strangers and good customer service, which Europeans often misinterpret as hypocritical, hence superficial. Ironically, in *Desperate Housewives*, horizontal interactions are the norm and vertical ones are considered taboo. When Rex pulled rank on his pharmacist, for instance, telling him that beautiful women like Bree preferred doctors to pharmacists, he created supercharged conflict for the American viewer. According to American norms, Rex should treat the customer exchange as a task conducted between social equals. For the European viewers I interviewed, though, Rex's pulling rank was nothing new, and while amusing, it wasn't very shocking.

As a rule, American service workers (as I was for many years) can afford to be friendly during customer service. They don't see themselves as social inferiors to the customer and so run little risk of losing face should they be criticized or ordered around. As Americans, they consider themselves individuals who can go back to school or get a better job if they want—both of which are less of an option in centralized, class-conscious Europe, where people are discouraged from entering new clans or venturing too far from their current ones.

Task vs. Relational Orientation

When Lynette began taking her kids' ADD medication in "Running to Stand Still" (1–6), she did so because she wanted to stay awake long enough to perform Herculean wifely tasks such as staying up all night to sew her kids' school play costumes and throwing a dinner party for Tom's colleagues. Her addiction and breakdown happened because she put pressure on herself to perform with the same energy and competence as a wife as she had in her high-powered executive position.

This American task-orientation is less common in Europe. Europeans are fond of saying they work to live, whereas Americans live to work, and there's some truth to this saying. But what isn't true is the corresponding European belief that task-oriented Americans are somehow more superficial than relational-oriented Europeans.

In the U.S., we work toward earning respect based on our performance. In Europe, on the other hand, one is respected not necessarily for what one does well, but for who one is by birth, rank, schooling and connections. This is the legacy of feudalism, which despite revolutions and comparatively new national borders still has a hold on European behavior and identity. As a result, when an American measures her worth according to task performance the way Lynette does, Europeans see the behavior as somehow inessential, as if Americans were acting like robots instead of human *beings*.

In Europe, if you want to get a job done, you need to have a good, almost clan-like relationship with your team, a team which is hard to join and hard to leave. It's difficult for Europeans to come together in quickly-formed, task-oriented groups whose members may or may not like each other. Americans, on the other hand, can more easily set aside their differences, stay individuated rather than fused in relation to the group and focus on the articulation of each member's task. Once the task is completed, American team members can then easily dissipate so that individuals can rearrange themselves into new teams to focus on new tasks.

This task-orientation, coupled with flexible individuality and the American tendency to identify explicit steps for creative projects rather than leave them implicit as many Europeans do, is a major factor contributing to America's worldwide competitive advantage across countless industries—including the entertainment industry.

It's no wonder then that shows like *Desperate Housewives* are able to get off the ground and wing their way around the world to popular and critical acclaim. *Desperate Housewives* was created by an individuated

American screenwriter whose mind lends itself to combining existing genre categories to create a brand-new category. Creator Marc Cherry also benefits from the American tradition of breaking down the art of storytelling into minute, articulated tasks, an explicit approach that allows him to work with a team of writers because writing tasks can be parsed out and assigned. (It's interesting to note in this connection that most screenwriting how-to books used in Europe have been translated from American English, and only very recently at that, since no such native tradition exists.) And when it comes to film production, American film crews are unparalleled in their ability to quickly pull together to get the job done, and to disperse just as quickly in readiness for the next project.

Out of One's Depth?

The question remains: if Europeans consider American behavior superficial, why do they enjoy American cultural products like *Desperate Housewives?*

According to German TV producer Vivien Bronner, for a television series to be successful it needs to have depth and universality. *Desperate Housewives* has both in spades. This is the main reason the show does so well in Europe. The other reason has to do with what art and literary critics call *ostranie*—a Russian word that means defamiliarization— which describes the basic enjoyment of any good art.

By universality and depth, Bronner does not mean complex philosophical abstractions that can only be understood by reading Heidegger at two A.M. while buzzed on No-Doze. She means TV fiction that provokes hope, pity and fear for characters whose basic needs are being challenged, needs which are independent of cultural conditioning. She calls these fiction building blocks *Basiskonflikte*, or basic conflicts, based on Abraham Maslow's hierarchy of human needs, which also serve as the foundation of depth psychology.

The more fundamental a need portrayed in TV fiction, the deeper the emotional response in the viewer, no matter what his or her culture. Maslow's five basic human needs are as follows: physiological needs (e.g., when Rex suffered food poisoning and a heart attack); safety needs (e.g., when the *Desperate Housewives* characters were threatened with murder, arson and burglary); need for love, affection and a sense of belonging (e.g., when Susan pursued Mike, when Bree tried to hold her family together, when Lynette tried to rekindle the spark in her marriage, when Zach longed for his late mother or when Edie befriended the desperate housewives); need for esteem (e.g., when Maisy felt rejected by neighborhood gossips, when Edie felt rejected by Mike and Susan, when Zach felt rejected by his father or when Lynette learned to respect her grumpy neighbor instead of throwing eggs at her); and the need for self-actualization (when Bree's daughter yearned to go to modeling school in New York or when Gabrielle created a charity fashion show).

According to Maslow, other levels of human need exist beyond these, but their fulfillment is only possible when the five basic needs are met. Further needs include the longing for understanding, aesthetic appreciation and spiritual fulfillment. While these last three may at first seem deeper than the need for belonging and survival, they actually create less depth of emotional response for the majority of TV viewers worldwide. In fact, TV producer Bronner claims she would decline to produce a series based on a character's search to become, say, a pop star, a painter or a priest, no matter how well-written the script. Such driving instincts, while admirable and inspiring, do not a create deep emotional resonance for most people, including *Desperate Housewives* fans like me and the Europeans I interviewed for this piece.

Stranger Than Fiction

Not that the aesthetic experience is absent from European enjoyment of the series. On the contrary, the very foreignness of *Desperate Housewives* deepens the European experience of the show, making its impact in a sense even deeper for Europeans than for Americans. This experience is what the Russian Formalist Skhlovsky described as *ostranie,* or making strange:

> The purpose of art is to impart the sensation of things as they are perceived and not as they are known. The technique of art is to make objects "unfamiliar," to make forms difficult, to increase the difficulty and length of perception because the process of perception is an aesthetic end in itself and must be prolonged (Skhlovsky 12).

Ostranie is akin to culture shock. Any tourist abroad will tell you the feeling. You walk around a foreign city with a sense that everything is familiar yet strange, the same but different, charming yet alienating, and therefore all the more fascinating. The effect is a disconnect between habitual ways of thinking and perceiving, and into this gap slip new impressions and new ways of perceiving.

European viewers of *Desperate Housewives* experience a similar double-duty response. As screenwriter and filmmaker Jørn Precht puts it, "There's a certain distance I feel when I watch *Desperate Housewives*. . . . It's like a fairy tale and I feel safe, on the outside looking in. Like in the process of dreaming. I look at things from a distanced point of view but still feel the emotions as if I was inside the characters. . . . [E]verything in the show looks different from Germany and the German television aesthetic, and of course different from real life."

Ostranie is also heightened for European fans because the television stations abroad dub the show instead of using subtitles. "You can't tell which regions the characters are from," says Precht. "They speak in this sort of standardized, generic ideal German, which makes the story world somehow artificial. . . . There is even a German stand-up comedian who makes fun of that artificial dubbed way of speaking."

Precht goes on to explain that compared with German filmmakers, Americans are good at creating TV with a larger-than-life stylized aesthetic that is closer to the way commercials look than to videotaped shows or to real life. In the case of *Desperate Housewives*, this larger-than-life aesthetic is purposely exaggerated. As a result, the inner contradiction between the show's faultless, glossy surface—as faultless and glossy as Bree's perfectly coiffed red hair—and the deeply faulted nature of the characters serves to deepen the show's appeal, not only for Americans, who of course also perceive the inherent contradiction, but even more so for Europeans, who experience an added layer of cross-cultural *ostranie*.

If, as Skhlovsky suggests, the effect of art is to heighten awareness by making the familiar seem unfamiliar, and so to free up the mind from habitual perceptions, then Europeans need not fear the dreaded Americanization of European culture. For it is in the very moment of cross-cultural contact that critical distance is born.

Conclusion

Desperate Housewives owes as much of its success overseas to American cultural patterns that emphasize individuation, innovation and horizontal expansion into the future as it does to its deeply universal themes that touch a chord for viewers regardless of culture. Add to this the extra element of fascination provided by cross-cultural difference, and the show's foreign appeal is complete.

Unfortunately, however, negative stereotypes about Americans co-exist with the show's success. We can only hope that continued cultural contact in both directions—via TV and movies, for starters—will help erode negative stereotypes. For in order to communicate interculturally, each side first needs to understand the other's differing assumptions. What happens after that is like magic. As we begin to see another culture from the inside, we see our own culture from the outside. We may lose a bit of our innocence in the process—that sense of one's own behavior as the natural and normal way—but what we gain is infinitely richer.

We gain new dimensions in time and space.

And the chance to live with other cultures in peace.

References

Baudry, Pascal. *Français et Américains: L'Autre Rive.* Paris: Village Mondial, 2004.

Bronner, Vivien. *Schreiben fürs Fernsehen.* Berlin: Autorenhaus Verlag, 2004.

Carrol, Raymonde. *Évidences Invisibles: Américains et Français au Quotidien.* Paris: Seuil, 1991.

Hall, Edward T. *The Hidden Dimension.* New York: Anchor, 1990.

Newberry, Sara, ed., *Desperate Housewives: Behind Closed Doors.* New York: Hyperion, 2005.

Schneider, Susan C., and Jean-Louis Barsoux. *Managing Across Cultures.* Upper Saddle River, NJ: Prentice Hall, 1997.

Skhlovsky, Victor. "Art as Technique." *Russian Formalist Criticism: Four Essays.* Eds. Lee T. Lemon and Marion J. Reis. Lincoln: University of Nebraska Press, 1965.

Stewart, Edward C. and Milton J. Bennet. *American Cultural Patterns: A Cross-Cultural Perspective.* Yarmouth, ME: Intercultural Press, 1991.

Novelist and screenwriter Deanna Carlyle identifies most with Edie the outsider on *Desperate Housewives,* although she would never go so far as to blackmail someone into being her friend! Deanna makes friends by creating clubs she'd like to join. She is co-founder of the International Women's Fiction Festival and originator of the popular online discussion group: Chick Lit: Women's Fiction Markets and Tips. To learn more about her fiction and non-fiction, visit www.deannacarlyle.com.

Jill Winters

The Lost Boys of Wisteria Lane

I wouldn't want to be involved with Bree, Lynette, Susan or Gabrielle. The men on Wisteria Lane can't seem to catch a break; if they aren't being admitted to the hospital for manufactured heart trouble or arrested for the accidental assault of gay men, they're being maneuvered out of promotions by their more Machiavellian wives or cuckolded by their underage gardeners. But, as Jill Winters demonstrates, they may only have themselves (and the skill of the Desperate Housewives *writing team) to blame.*

BY ITS VERY TITLE, *Desperate Housewives* is a show about women and men. The word "housewife" comes loaded with not only the female it references, but by implication, her male counterpart. Yet the title is deceptive. The female protagonists of *Desperate Housewives* are not actually desperate, at least not in any lasting sense of the word. And the male characters are not actually counterparts as much as they are irritants—and inferior opponents. In fact, the men on Wisteria Lane are utterly ineffectual, especially in their inability to get what they want in both the short and long term.

If you look at season one as a story, you will see that over the course of its narrative arc, each male character fails to achieve what he wants—and what he wants more than anything is mastery over his immediate situation, which includes the woman in his life. He never gets it. Rather, whatever power and influence he appears to possess at the beginning of the story proves illusory. The question is why.

Why do the men fail? Are the external forces working against them too great to surmount? Or are the men simply less manipulative or less *deft* at manipulation than the women?

No. At the heart of the matter, each man is ineffectual because of a fundamental weakness in his character, and that is his inability to actualize what he represents.

Each of the five major male characters—Rex, Carlos, Tom, Mike and John—has a particular way of asserting his masculinity. He has a specific brand of strength and efficacy—or rather, he *appears* to—but like any weak construction, his self-identity eventually collapses, leaving little more than a defeated heap in its place. Interestingly, the exact traits that define each man's masculinity at the beginning of the story are inverted by the end, becoming not only the symbols of his ineffectuality, but the tools of his emasculation.

Caveat: I'm one of those annoying people who believe that everything's a construct, so before we go any further, let's first identify our terms. For our purposes, "masculinity" will refer to the confidence that comes with strength, power and ability. "Emasculation" will refer to the negating, invalidating or disintegrating of that confidence.

The Masochist and the Mama's Boy

Rex Van de Kamp and Carlos Solis both swagger around Wisteria Lane using perhaps the most clichéd measure of masculine prowess: money. *Status.* But just as status is, at its root, a contrivance, so is what it attempts to project.

Affluence is crucial to the way Rex and Carlos portray themselves. When his family was at its most divisive, Rex sought the respect of his children by buying them lavish gifts (a new car for his son, modeling school for his daughter). When Carlos' wife told him she wanted more romance, he responded the only way he knew how—by buying her first an expensive necklace, then a sports car. In both cases, financial power allowed these men more than just position in the home; it also gave them a sense of stability—a kind of reassurance of each one's masculinity. But money cannot buy strength of character, the only real stability one can have.

Over the course of the story, Rex and Carlos go from big-shot heads of household to ineffectual weaklings. This transition, while dramatic, is actually quite unsurprising given the chinks in each man's character, evident right at the onset. By the end of season one, not only have Rex and Carlos lost social respectability, but they have also come to rely on their wives literally for their survival.

Rex in brief: A relatively handsome, middle-aged doctor. He tells his wife of almost twenty years that he wants a divorce. They try counseling, but ultimately separate. What brings them back together, however, is Rex's heart attack—which he has in the throes of one of his regular S&M sessions with the neighborhood socialite-turned-recreational-prostitute. As Rex's wife, Bree, nurses her husband back to health, she also nurses a fierce grudge over his infidelity, and a hatred for his perversions—even as she tries to dabble in them herself to please him. With a tense love-hate dynamic, Rex and Bree attempt to salvage their marriage, all the while unaware that George, their pharmacist, who is in love with Bree, has been tampering with Rex's heart pills. Rex has a second heart attack and dies soon afterward.

Brilliantly, just as *Desperate Housewives* depicted its male characters at their most confident and commanding in the first episode, it also provided clues for the precariousness of that confidence. In the first episode, after Rex told Bree that he wanted a divorce, she fixed him a salad with onions, to which he was fatally allergic, and he ended up in a hospital bed. In this one incident the power dynamic was reversed; Bree was the one who was dumped, but just as swiftly, Rex became the wounded party.

From here, things unfolded. We learned that Rex routinely cried during sex. And then, shortly into season one, that he wanted to hire a sex surrogate, because he was too insecure and embarrassed to tell his wife what he wanted in bed. In fact, when Bree pressed Rex on the issue he became so self-conscious and flustered that he stormed out like a child.

Later, an amusing yet symbolic incident occurred on the golf course—a distinctly affluent and male-dominated territory. In an argument about marijuana, Bree threw a cupful of their son's urine on Rex. I am hard-pressed to think of something more degrading than that. She left him standing there—soaked, soiled and emasculated among his fellow doctors.

But this emasculation was nothing compared to the revelation that followed. Rex finally confessed to his wife what he desired sexually and that was to be beaten, whipped and stepped on (Bree was appropriately appalled). At this point, it was obvious that the scriptwriters were in on the joke. Masculine strength and power can be inverted at any time, and taken to the opposite extreme.

Then Rex had a heart attack and Bree rushed to his side. Having just discovered his infidelity, she leaned over his hospital bed and vowed to "eviscerate" him in divorce court. A feeble, speechless Rex just lay there, helplessly.

Yet, his only saving grace *was* Bree, who proceeded to take care of him rather than eviscerate him. At this point, the reversal of his position in their marriage was blatant. While the story might've begun with Rex casting Bree aside, it would end with him relying solely on her for his recovery.

In an attempt to reassert his masculinity, Rex then tried to intimidate George, a competitor for Bree's affections. Predictably, Rex fell back on his usual crutch: using his affluence and status to assert himself as the dominant male. With blatant mockery, he told George that women like Bree would always end up with doctors, not pharmacists.

But his momentary satisfaction was costly. Not only did he fail to dissuade George from pursuing Bree, but he also made a deadly enemy. George—who responded by telling Rex that he was "not a nice person" (understatement of the year)—set in motion a plan to kill him.

Not only was Rex ineffectual when it came to intimidating a rival, but he became ineffectual in his marriage; after telling Bree that he didn't want her seeing George anymore she went behind his back and told George that Rex would have no say in their friendship.

As Rex grew sicker, he became even weaker and more dependent on Bree. Here, *Desperate Housewives* exhibited its dark comic streak more darkly than ever. Rex, who began season one as a doctor, ended up on the opposite side of the medical spectrum, as an invalid. His masculinity had been wholly inverted; his emasculation was complete.

Also relying on status for his entire self-identity is Carlos, who had acquired a fortune working in business and a hot trophy wife to go with it.

Carlos in brief: A domineering and wealthy businessman. He appears to have it all—except a faithful wife. Convinced that Gabrielle is cheating on him, and consumed by jealousy, Carlos targets the wrong man, not once but twice, and also calls in his mother to spy for him. His jealousy takes a backseat, though, to his legal and financial problems once he's arrested for embezzlement. Claiming innocence, he pleads with his wife to burn incriminating documents that he's hidden, which indicates to Gabrielle that her husband is actually guilty. That, plus the fact that Carlos has successfully tampered with Gabrielle's birth control pills to get her pregnant, puts him at the top of her shit list. When season one ends, Carlos is in jail, after having pled guilty—something he only did because Gabrielle swore she would leave him if he drained their coffers any longer pursuing his defense. His suspicions have been confirmed about his wife's infidelity, yet all Carlos has left to cling to is his marriage.

As with Rex, the first episode of *Desperate Housewives* presented Carlos with a kind of brimming confidence while at the same time undercutting it. Carlos took Gabrielle to a work party, where Gabrielle feared that Carlos' boss, Tanaka, would spend the whole evening trying to grope her. Unapologetically, Carlos told her just to suck it up, because Tanaka was his boss and they shouldn't offend him. Here, Carlos' brown-nosing intruded on his bravado, making it hard not to see him as weak rather than masculine.

Despite this, when Carlos began to suspect that Gabrielle was cheating on him, he was fiercely jealous. Not knowing what to do, he asked his mother to come visit so she could spy on Gabrielle and report back to Carlos. At this point it bears considering that, bluster and bossy personality aside, Carlos is more of a mama's boy than a man. To bolster that notion, the scriptwriters painted Juanita Solis as staunchly overprotective—even dangerously so. With a veiled threat she confided to Gabrielle that *she* killed Carlos' abusive father a long time ago, and would kill again if it meant protecting her boy.

In spite of his attempts to control his marriage, Carlos constantly found himself at his wife's mercy. When he was arrested, he told her to burn incriminating papers, but she deliberately held on to them. When Carlos was back at home under house arrest, a ticked-off Gabrielle took their dinner and walked across the street to eat it—still in Carlos' view—so as to remind him that she was in control, not him. Later, he begged her to lie for him in court, but before she agreed she made several demands of her own.

Here, again, the darkly comic tone of *Desperate Housewives* was evident. After toying with the tenuous nature of masculinity, the show turned it on its head and deftly exposed the ineffectuality that lay beneath.

Time and time again, it was a snap for Gabrielle to outsmart Carlos. And if that weren't emasculating enough, whenever Carlos—for lack of any other recourse—tried brute force, he *still* failed to get what he wanted. He beat up not one, but two gay men, wrongly thinking they were having an affair with his wife (all the while missing the real lover, his gardener, who had been under his nose the whole time).

When Carlos couldn't convince Gabrielle to sign a post-nuptial agreement any other way, he physically forced her to put her signature on the document. His victory was short-lived, however, when she told him in no uncertain terms that if he didn't tear it up, she would not be waiting for him when he got out of jail. Considering that nearly everything Carlos did in the first season was tied into trying to keep and control Gabrielle, he really had no choice but to back down. In fact, the only reason he made her sign the post-nuptial agreement in the first place was to keep her from leaving him. This was revealing in and of itself. Carlos' self-worth was so tied up in his financial status that he truly could not fathom any reason for Gabrielle to stay married to him without it.

At the beginning of the story, Carlos exuded the kind of confidence that comes with money, and truly we see that money was his only measure of his own masculinity. And brilliantly, it was his greed that kick-started his emasculating demise. Once he was arrested for embezzlement, Carlos began a downward spiral of slipping control and dwindling finances. Understandably, he clung to the last scraps of money that he had, even bartering with Gabrielle from jail in the beginning of season two for control over their checkbook (unsurprisingly, she won that power struggle, too), because in every other way he'd proven ineffectual.

We were given a very different picture of Carlos at the beginning of season two than we were at the beginning of season one. Slumped in an orange jumpsuit with a resigned stamp of misery on his face, Carlos began season two a weak, bitter man: insecure, jealous, corrupt and not intelligent or original enough to do much about it. With his mother dead and his neediness and vulnerability transposed onto his wife, he depended on Gabrielle not only to visit, but to do him favors "on the outside" that would keep him from getting beaten up by his fellow inmates.

Carlos' new reality at the beginning of season two is perversely humorous, especially in the stark way it contrasts with the bravado of his beginning. At one point Carlos even said to Gabrielle, "We're not very nice people," but it certainly wasn't a true epiphany or an indication of any significant personal growth on his part. Rather, the admission came from a defeated place inside him; it came from a bested man, who holds no power and knows it, and now must slump over and accept it.

The Lame Duck

Let's talk about Tom—who, by the way, is so ineffectual that I'm constantly forgetting his name and having to refer to him as "you know, Matt from *Melrose Place*."

Tom in brief: An affable working dad. Tom has a fairly successful career in advertising, while his wife Lynette stays home to take care of their four children. As season one progresses, Lynette's discontentment with home life and Tom's long hours inspire her to get Tom's promotion withdrawn. Through a series of subsequent machinations, Lynette unwittingly drives Tom to quit his firm in protest. With Tom unemployed, he and Lynette switch roles; she returns to the advertising world and he decides to stay home with the kids.

I hate to bash Tom Scavo because the truth is he is a dream husband. He's supportive, easygoing, inexplicably adores his nagging wife and actually seems to enjoy spending time with their rotten, disrespectful children. On top of that, he is both comfortable and eager in his role as breadwinner and provider for his wife and family.

Really, what's not to love?

But of course, likeability has nothing to do with strength or efficacy. Take Tom's wife, Lynette: arguably the most selfish character on the show, she is also the most swiftly efficient at getting what she wants. Tom is not so fortunate. In fact, he suffers from the two-pronged curse of being too nice and barely competent.

The scriptwriters of *Desperate Housewives* paint Tom as the quintessential husband and father, and then undercut him by depicting him as inadequate for the role. Again, there were early signs of his ineffectuality. At a dinner party, Tom's boss was far more impressed by Lynette's marketing ideas than Tom's. Despite Tom's long hours and his eagerness, he was ultimately unable to excel at his particular brand of masculinity—being the breadwinner—because despite his work ethic, he simply wasn't as talented as others in his field, including his own wife.

While Tom's descent into uselessness did not end on such a dramatic note as jail or death, it was still an unequivocal emasculation. After quitting his job in frustration, he surrendered his role as breadwinner, telling Lynette that she could have what she'd wanted all along—to go back to work—while he stayed home to raise the kids.

There was something so pathetic about Tom's acquiescence. Was it that easy to extinguish his fire? Where was the drive? Where was the courage, the confidence? And after learning that Lynette was the one who got his promotion revoked, did Tom stand up for himself? Did he make a stance against her betrayal? Did he assert any authority in their home or establish any equality in their marriage?

Did he command any respect whatsoever?

No. Instead, Tom pretty much shriveled. Sure he sulked a little, but ultimately, he freely handed over his dream of a successful career.

But Tom's ineffectuality didn't end there. When season two began, we saw him failing at his new role of househusband, too. The house was a mess and Tom seemed unwilling to be diligent about cleaning. Fittingly, Lynette chastised him, and when that wasn't enough of an incentive, she fell back on her usual strategy: manipulation. She put a rat in their house so Tom would find it and realize just how bad he was at keeping house. Unsurprisingly, it worked like a charm and Tom fell into line. Now Tom could rest assured—he was incompetent at work and at home. To drive this point home further, he threw his back out one morning so Lynette had to take their baby to work with her, while Tom lay uselessly on the floor.

Although Tom is a nice guy and a decent husband, he is also a wholly ineffectual male. And once he lost the masculine identity he'd constructed for himself—as the breadwinner—all his confidence crumbled, along with his relevance in his own home.

Pretty and Dumb (and Dumber)

Throughout season one, Mike Delfino and John (who was apparently so ineffectual he didn't even get a last name until halfway through the first season) both served similar purposes on the show: to provide sex appeal. Both were handsome and muscular, and, when all is said and done, not much else.

John in brief: A senior in high school who works part time as a gardener. He is having an affair with a married Gabrielle and has mistaken their mutual infatuation for a lasting relationship. Gabrielle ends the affair after John's parents find out about it, but at the height of her difficulties with her husband, Carlos, starts it up again. John believes he's in love with Gabrielle and that she will leave Carlos if only John has more money, so he works and saves to try to win her. Ultimately he is the one to tell Carlos about their affair, and Gabrielle breaks it off again.

Mike in brief: The handsome, elusive "plumber" with a private agenda. He is trying to uncover what happened to his girlfriend, Deirdre, who disappeared twelve years earlier, and somehow his investigation has led him to Wisteria Lane. Despite Mike's secrecy and desire to keep a low profile, he quickly becomes enamored of single mom Susan, who lives across the street. The two become involved. Mike futilely tries to keep his past private, but Susan doggedly uncovers it piece by piece. Eventually Mike confronts his neighbor, Paul, and accuses him of Deirdre's murder. He also learns that Paul's son, Zach, was Deirdre's child and might very well be his, too.

I will talk briefly about John and Mike; considering what one-note, two-dimensional characters they were in the first season of *Desperate Housewives*, brevity is only appropriate. Sure, I could go on about how the show was up to its old tricks—presenting shades of masculinity and cleverly undercutting them. I could talk about how John paraded around bare-chested most of the time, yet had such childlike naiveté, it was impossible to see him as a grown man. Muscles aside, he was just a boy—and with his fresh-scrubbed youthfulness, his boyishly inquisitive eyes and the fact that he called his married lover "Mrs. Solis," the viewer could never see him as anything else.

But no matter what, John's age contributed greatly to his gullibility. It wasn't a matter of stupidity, but inexperience. So what was Mike's excuse?

At first glance Mike seemed quietly intelligent, brooding and reticent. But upon closer inspection, you could see that it was the brooding and reticence that made him *appear* intelligent—not his actions. The masculinity Mike projected came from two basic things: one, his hunky appearance, and two, his persona as the Enigmatic Loner. Unfortunately, both are equally superficial and only served to mask his ineffectuality.

Simply put, Mike lacked the skill to accomplish what he wanted. Yes, he *eventually* figured out that Paul was involved in Deirdre's death, and he *eventually* confronted him. But what on earth took him so long? Why didn't he know Deirdre had a child? Didn't whatever trail Mike followed to Wisteria Lane also clue him in on the baby—a.k.a. the one and only reason Paul would have had to harm Deirdre in the first place?

This might have been the fault of his two-dimensional characterization, but the fact remains: Mike's "investigation" was something less than stellar. In fact, nosy Mrs. Tilman was a far sharper, better sleuth;

she figured the whole mystery out way before Mike. She also took *action* before Mike—making him seem impotent rather than masculine, passive rather than effectual.

To impugn Mike's Enigmatic Alpha Male bit even more was the unimpressive course of his relationship with Susan. Susan is oh so cutesy and klutzy and apparently has the power to bring Mike to his knees no matter what she does—including snooping through his things and waffling back and forth about whether or not she trusts him. The fact that Susan's drama-queen antics impacted often on Mike's behavior and distracted him thoroughly from his so-called investigation doesn't speak well for his effectiveness. Season two began on very much the same note. Mike had a new mystery to solve (finding his son, Zach), and Susan was blowing hot and cold again. But as expected, Mike was pretty much stagnating on both fronts, spinning his wheels and affecting the posture of the Strong Silent Type. Sadly, it was even less convincing the second time around.

The Almost Effectual Male

A word about Paul Young—who, in my mind, gets an unfair rap as a psycho nut-job. Murderous past aside, Paul is the only man on Wisteria Lane who came *close* to achieving what he wanted. With his singular focus and shrewd determination, he was almost always a step ahead of his meddling neighbors. He was driven to the point of being almost fearless. Indeed his only fear was losing his son, and he would do whatever was necessary to prevent that from happening.

While he might have lied to the people around him, Paul's *personal* behavior was driven by the utmost sincerity. Swiftly and without hesitation, he avenged his wife's death (by killing her blackmailer, Mrs. Huber), and set about protecting the secret they shared (that Mary Alice killed Deirdre twelve years earlier and he had helped her cover it up). But try as Paul did, in the end he failed. And he failed because of the ineffectuality that haunted his past—the weakness of character that allowed him to go along with a situation he wasn't, and would never have been, equipped to handle.

Desperation as Character

Taken as a whole, *Desperate Housewives* applies its desperation differently to its characters. Any desperation the women might feel is transitory; it pertains to specific obstacles that arise, which they inevitably push past. For the men of Wisteria Lane, desperation becomes *who* they are. It truly characterizes them once they fail to achieve what they want, and their illusion of power and influence breaks down.

Female machinations cannot be blamed for the men's failures, but they *are* key—key for setting the scene in which the ineffectual male brings about his own demise.

The biggest difference between *Desperate Housewives'* male and female characters is stability. The women are stable characters, but the men change—change, but not grow. Rather, their sense of self is so weakly rooted that they devolve instead of evolve—each one inevitably crippled by his own ineptitude.

Now that's dark comedy.

Jill Winters is a Phi Beta Kappa, summa cum laude graduate of Boston College with a degree in history. She has taught women's studies, and is the author of five romantic mystery novels, including *Just Peachy*, *Raspberry Crush*, *Blushing Pink* and *Plum Girl*, which was a finalist for the Dorothy Parker Award of Excellence. Jill also contributed an original essay to the non-fiction anthology *Flirting with Pride and Prejudice*. Her latest book, *Lime Ricky*, is in stores now. (Jill's also happy to add that she is nothing like anyone on Wisteria Lane, although she'd love a friend like Bree.) Visit her online at http://www.jillwinters.com.

Sarah Zettel

Something Familiar, Something Peculiar
Why Men Love *Desperate Housewives*

For a show ostensibly for and about women, Desperate Housewives *has an awful lot of male viewers. About half, actually, and they're not all watching for Nicollette Sheridan's cleavage or because their wives or girlfriends are making them. But as Jill Winters showed, the men of* Desperate Housewives *are hardly worth envying. So what's the appeal? Sarah Zettel's got it all figured out.*

W ELL. MY GOODNESS.

It seems everybody hates *Desperate Housewives*.

They hate it because it's full of sex, and violence, with a dash of violent sex thrown in. They hate it because they think women should not blame men for what are patently their own failings. They hate it because it suggests that the two-parent nuclear family might not always be perfect, and that its failings might not be entirely the neglectful woman's fault.

Mostly, the critical crowd hates it because everybody but them loves *Desperate Housewives*. And why shouldn't they? The show succeeds on a number of levels. Some of them are basic TV look-and-feel levels: It's a pretty, well-shot show. It also succeeds at genuinely entertaining storytelling, and this has been pointed out by sharper pens than mine. What seems to have caught everybody off-guard, however, is that many of the most avid watchers are...men.

How can this possibly be? After all, the show is entirely about how the stupid, Neanderthalish males have screwed up the lives of the poor women, and how those poor women must struggle against these thoughtless, brutish men.

Right?

Actually, no. The storied dish that *Desperate Housewives* serves up has a sauce that works as well for the gander as it does for the goose.

Superior storytelling is difficult, and it is complicated. For a story to deliver long-term entertainment, it's got to do a number of things all at once. Now, I'm talking pure entertainment storytelling here, not art. It's got to provide sympathetic characters, an accessible storyline and a safe pressure-valve for the audience's emotions, even—or perhaps most particularly—their socially unacceptable emotions.

Desperate Housewives does all this, and a little bit more. That it provides plenty of eye-candy for both sexes and multiple orientations is immediately obvious. Ditto on possession-voyeurism, with beautiful cars and houses as well as clothes and jewelry.

There is also the heavy slapstick component to the show. The humor is very (you should excuse the expression) broad. Susan runs naked through the bushes while trying to get back into her house (talk about a selling point for a male audience!). Gabrielle frantically tries to conceal evidence of her latest rendezvous. George attempts to steal a kiss and ends up shooting off his toe. It's bawdy, loud, raucous, wince-inducing humor. In the words of the old song, "nothing pretentious or polite."

While we're speaking of bawdy, and things that appeal to men, I think this show sets a new record for the most cleavage revealed by a network, and in these days of Fox TV, that takes some doing. Even uptight Bree can't get away from scoop necks or cut-out sweaters, and the supposedly dowdy Lynette doesn't seem to realize that Oxford shirts come with three buttons above the nipple-line.

The storylines are also slanted to appeal to the male as well as the female viewer. There are relationship stories here, the stock and trade of women's literature and the romance genre, but these actually take a backseat to the elements of suspense. There's only one love story here, the developing relationship between Susan and Mike. The major storylines are all mystery and suspense. We are dealing in murder, intrigue and mayhem, and men chained up in basements. Physical peril is immediate, action is present in every episode, and it is visceral.

The writing is not only bawdy, and suspenseful, but also flat-out clever. In fact, one of the most memorable and funniest scenes was tidy, anal-retentive Bree just talking about how much she likes sex. The character dialogue is full of perfectly worded comebacks, lovely turns of phrase and deadly verbal cuts. You know, all the things we ourselves wish we could come up with at cocktail parties or business meetings.

If this were the beginning and the end of it, I don't think the show would appeal as much to either men or women. So far, these are all the elements of a good but fairly basic soap opera. *Desperate Housewives* goes on to accomplish two tasks that could be mutually contradictory, but which the show manages to synch together in a formula that works smoothly and makes use of the basic elements of American culture.

Fifty years ago, the legend goes, on the day Japan surrendered and World War II ended, Rosie the Riveter joyfully threw away her overalls and bandanna. She moved away from all her relatives into a detached house with a big grassy yard in the suburbs. There, she settled down into her true identity as June Cleaver. In this persona, she capably and lovingly cared for every emotional and physical aspect of the lives of her husband and children (and kept to her budget). She never again desired anything except the occasional afternoon coffee party and a new string of pearls on important anniversaries.

For fifty years the media and the social myth they bolster has told us the above scenario is *Normal*, with a capital N. Every Normal woman not only wants this life more than anything else, but women who don't get it go slightly to severely nuts and cannot be truly happy. Oh, and Normal women can handle all the responsibility perfectly. It's what they're meant for.

Never mind that somehow the daughters of all those June Roses grew up to burn their bras, get advanced degrees and move into the workforce. That isn't Normal. Normal is housewifery and lovely success at housewifery. We've been told that for almost fifty years.

But *Desperate Housewives* dares to suggest that maybe the life of the June Rose isn't entirely normal. It's hard. It's complicated. Failure is not only possible, but success is desperately hard, and might make you just as crazy as spinsterhood was supposed to.

But the show does more than that. While on the surface *Desperate Housewives* points out that women struggle with the failure of their partners to live their roles in the Great American Myth, it is equally about the men struggling with the women's failures.

You see, the Great American Myth goes on to tell us that same day Rosie morphed into June, G.I. Joe marched in the door (whole and sane, of course, because WWII was a *good* war), donned a gray flannel suit (the pipe was optional) and purposefully, contentedly settled into his adult life as Ward Cleaver. Ward's only obligations were to provide monetary support for his family and protect them from such suburban threats as might brush the edges of the lawn he mowed on Saturdays. Oh, and to remember to buy the pearls for those important anniversaries, and maybe roses. As with June Rose, we have been told that Joe Ward's life is normal, and easy, because it's what comes naturally to every adult male of decent character.

Except, of course, his isn't easy or simple any more than hers is, and *Desperate Housewives* takes that on.

All the husbands on *Desperate Housewives* try hard to provide for and protect their families, even (before his death) Rex. Somehow, though, it's never enough. They cannot protect the individuals in their families from their own failings. They cannot even protect themselves. Despite their best efforts, the men remain vulnerable to their personal failures, and the severe failings of their wives. This speaks to the complexity and confusion of men's lives in the modern middle class. Men, like women, have been sold a mythical bill of goods that has turned out to be a little less than promised, and with all the different families on the show, the male viewers, like the female viewers, get to pick the struggles with which they most sympathize.

We've got Rex, who got perfection and found out it wasn't what he wanted. There's Paul, so desperately trying to protect what he loves, and failing. He bought a baby to make his wife happy. He cleaned up after the murder his wife committed in order to keep his family together. But not even murder was enough to keep his son with him.

There's also Tom, who is the one who tries the hardest to do what is needed, not just what is expected, and still finds himself at the end of his rope. Through Tom, the difficulties of the domestic sphere are illuminated for men. Tom really does his best to be a good husband and father, yet he is tricked, manipulated and unfairly accused by Lynette. He was even clocked in the jaw by his wife (although I was fully in favor of that one). He's loving yet long-suffering. This makes the whole situation classically sympathetic for men. Husbands love wives and wives love husbands, but managing a marriage and a household is hard work, and everybody gets tired now and again, and wants to bitch over a cup of coffee or a mug of beer.

Then there's Carlos. Carlos ought to be an alpha male. He's physically powerful and has a dominant presence. He's made a pile of money and acquired a gorgeous woman to go with his host of other beautiful possessions. And he still somehow ended up cuckolded and jailed.

Carlos' story illustrates another reason for men to like *Desperate*

Housewives. One little-discussed reason people enjoy certain forms of entertainment is that they are allowed to feel superior to the characters before them.

Here's Carlos: powerful, richer than Midas, a mover and a shaker. The male watcher can experience his story and imagine how *he* would do so much better. He would be a superior lover and caretaker for the beautiful Gabrielle. The watcher would also be smart enough to make a pile in business, and either have done so without breaking the law or would have blown the whistle on his unscrupulous partner.

But *Desperate Housewives* goes even further. It allows men a vicarious outlet for emotions it is not socially acceptable for them to admit, and it does this through the many sons on the show. The sons are victims in these storylines. They are victims of their parents' failings. They are helpless and sometimes hopeless. They are groping and flailing, trying to find their ways, thrust into adult situations they can't handle and getting burned by the fires their fathers, as well as their mothers, set.

We all know how it was to feel that way. Everybody feels helpless as a teenager, and as an adult. We get confused between the requirements of our real lives and the expectations of society, both real and imagined. Women can talk about this, out loud and with each other. Men have no socially acceptable outlet for such feelings. Our society allows men to get angry, but not frightened. They certainly cannot admit they are powerless. Showing the sons as victims not only arouses the protective instincts in men, but allows them a vicarious, safe and sympathetic outlet for the feelings of powerlessness that affect so many of us, men and women, in complex and high-pressure times.

And, by the way, I am including John the Gardener on the list of victimized sons. John is the embodiment of the most famous young-male fantasy: gorgeous older woman wants you for sex. Lots and lots of sex. Yet, it was made clear that John was Gabrielle's victim. She manipulated him from the get-go, and each time he tried to assert a little control over his situation, she outmaneuvered him. Gabrielle would only have him on her terms, and though he tried hard, there was nothing he could do to change that.

The apple we see tossed around in the opening credits is important. All these women are on some level male fantasy objects, but they are dangerous fantasies. *Desperate Housewives* tells men to be very, very careful what they wish for, but in a way that entertains rather than preaches.

This leads to the secret of *Desperate Housewives* that appeals to men as much as women, and has completely eluded the critics who are shocked at the sex. It's the other half of that complex and outwardly contradictory combination I was talking about before.

Desperate Housewives is an intensely, and conventionally, moral show. When the characters, male and female, fail to follow the dictates of conventional morality they get into increasingly hot water. The audience, men and women alike, observes the downfall of the unvirtuous and is able to take comfort in their own personal morality in the real world.

Take Rex. Rex was the little boy who did not want to grow up. He wanted all his "needs" fulfilled, but did not want to have to take any responsibility. His marriage failed when he not only did not tell his wife what he wanted, he cheated on her and still wouldn't acknowledge any fault. His irresponsible and immoral actions led directly to his death. Could there be a clearer criticism of a behavior in the storyteller's lexicon?

Yet, like Carlos' failings, Rex's struck a chord with the watcher. We are all familiar with the popular American myth that boys really do not want to grow up. As single young men, they are free to drink, wander and chase girls (and not shave, clean or bathe) as they choose. Who would want to give that up?

This, however, is not a socially useful state. So when stories are told about such young men, they generally end with the young man voluntarily shouldering his long neglected duty, and liking it—usually because he's in love. Men who do not grow up are either ridiculed or come to bad ends, like Rex. So the male viewer gets to feel validated in his own choice to fully shoulder his necessary burdens.

You'll notice something else about the show, in terms of its portrayals of men and women. When women on the show commit violence, they commit suicide. They turn the violence inward. Men, on the other hand, turn it outward. They commit murder. Even here, the show stays comfortably within the bounds of traditional perception and myth.

This is the *Desperate Housewives* theme: The story shows a fantasy—wealth, sex, various aspects of physical and material perfection—and then shows the viewer how they are better off without it. Like *People* magazine and its sibling publications, it provides a look at what we are all supposed to desire and then allows us to be content with what we have, because we're really better people than the ones we see in the slick images.

And, of course, no discussion of the appeal of *Desperate Housewives* could be concluded without examining that ultimate male fantasy character, Mike.

Oh, stop looking at me like that. He is too.

Mike is the show's James Bond, guaranteed to appeal to both men and women. He's ruggedly handsome. He's also the only man in the series who has no ties; he's very much a lone wolf. Like a hero out of a Clint Eastwood western, he rode into town to do a job, and found that job more than he bargained for. He's the object of desire of beautiful women. He's hyper-competent in basic manly skills such as plumbing. He can throw a punch and shoot a gun and does not fear to kill when he must. He longs for love, but has to remain aloof. He's relentlessly true to his mission and his personal morality, and will not let a little thing like burgeoning love for a beautiful woman get in the way. As a result, he suffers for his morality, and this renders him noble. And—bonus!—he's that evergreen TV hero, the single dad. He will do anything to protect his wayward son, and unlike the other men on the show, he tends to be successful at what he sets out to do.

The thing that is most interesting about Mike is he's unique in the cast of characters. On this show which is supposed to be for and about women, Mike has no female analogue. There is no unambiguous, unattached female hero to match him. Remember when I said the show was really very traditional? This is another example. There can be no female Mike. Traditional social structure and American myth do not allow for it. Women don't get road stories (unless they're going to drive off the edge of the Grand Canyon at the end), not even in a show that is as full of surface shock as *Desperate Housewives*.

By adhering to this aspect of our traditional myth structure, *Desperate Housewives* does something I like rather less about the show, but which renders it safe for a mass, male viewing audience: It tacitly affirms that men are superior to women. Unattached women on the show are represented by two figures. First there's Edie, who, while she is given a background that renders her somewhat sympathetic, is hardly anybody's hero. Then there's Mrs. Huber, a blackmailer who gets what's coming to her at the hands of a murderous man. In the middle of the ambiguity, the vulnerability and the double-edged swords of all the fantasies involving women, we see here that only an unattached male is capable of unwavering morality. Only this lone male can fully and capably protect his child (unless a frightened woman interferes, of course). Only a man can move freely, depend solely on himself and walk away from love that compromises his noble nature. Mike is the only fantasy on the show with no downside. Oh, sure, he's heartbroken, but that's only tempered his nature and made him surer of himself as opposed to shattering him.

Desperate Housewives is a complicated show. It has a number of interwoven, ongoing storylines. It's a combination of light shock value, comfortable grousing and a bit of airing of dirty laundry, but with rock-solid American cultural myth as its ultimate foundation. It appeals to a wide range of viewers because there is so much going on that you can safely and reliably pull from it whatever personal confirmation you want.

Even if you're a guy.

Sarah Zettel was born in Sacramento, California. Since then she has lived in ten cities, four states, two countries and become an author of a dozen science fiction and fantasy books, a host of short stories and novellas, as well as a handful of essays about pop culture in which she finds herself immersed. She lives in Michigan with her husband Tim, son Alexander and cat Buffy the Vermin Slayer, and when not writing, she drinks tea, gardens, practices tai chi and plays the fiddle, but not all at once. Sarah Zettel sincerely hopes she never in any way comes to resemble any of the characters seen on this show, but she would like their household incomes.

Acknowledgments

Many thanks to Amanda Lane of *Ultimate Desperate Housewives* (http://dh.ahaava.com) for her assistance with this manuscript.